OUR STORY

So Far

OUR STORY
So Far

Notes from the first 75 years of 3M Company

Published by
Minnesota Mining and Manufacturing Company
St. Paul, Minnesota, U.S.A.

Foreword

"Our Story" is about a company of men and women of enterprise, enthusiasm and innovation who develop themselves while working to fill the needs of others.

It is also a story of earlier 3M people who overcame adversity and carried their company from Two Harbors to St. Paul, from the width and breadth of the United States to six continents.

In 3M's 75th anniversary year it seems appropriate to record these accomplishments, not only to preserve a proud heritage but also to gain inspiration for the future.

The pages that follow cover only some of those events which today's perspective suggests are significant; they focus on just a few of the many employees, past and present, who participated—not just because they are exceptional people, but even more because they are typical of all 3M people.

"Our Story" is not a simple chronology, nor is it complete. New and exciting chapters are still being written by 80,000 of us.

It is to these 80,000—and to the thousands who preceded them—that "Our Story" is dedicated.

The Editors
August, 1977

Contents

A world at work

From Australia to Oslo, from Sao Paulo
to St. Paul, 3M people help set the rhythms
of business, commerce and industry

June 23, 1977: The day began, as all days do, in mid-Pacific just west of the international dateline. And 3M Company on this 75th anniversary date of its formation was part of the gradually gathering momentum of a world at work. The tempo of a new day's commercial and industrial activity was picked up first in New Zealand and Australia.

It was fair and cool, the second day of winter in the foothills of the Blue Mountains an hour west of Sydney as 3M Australia opened for business.

Abrasive-maker shift foreman Alan Fowler and tape group secretary Kathy Nesbitt were still receiving congratulations on their completion of 10 years service with 3M, and co-workers of David W. Gay, industrial engineering manager, were planning a suitable observance of his 20th anniversary with the company. Lorraine Mills, telephone operator at the St. Marys plant, had a birthday that day, too, but unlike 3M she chose not to reveal her age.

The third in a series of employee-management feedback sessions was convened for warehouse, materials handling and manufacturing staff services personnel by Ray Saunders, manager. Under examination was the role of distribution in the conduct of 3M's businesses.

A plant-wide safety drive to achieve one million accident-free work hours saw 3M Australia's receiving department add to its good record with the completion of 19 consecutive months without a lost-time accident.

Senior cost analyst John Psaltis was especially pleased with the 17-degree weather (that's lower 60s, Fahrenheit). By day's end he had been named outstanding player of a match in which the 3M employees rugby club trounced a Maritime Services Board team 13-3. Scorers for 3M, in this most important game of the season, included Mick Burdon, Tony Beilby and Ron Compton.

Far to the north and slightly west, safety was also in the thoughts, that day, of Tatsuo Watanabe, group general manager at Sumitomo 3M in Japan. He had just reported a substantial sale of 100,000 sets of shoe reflectors for 6 million yen ($22,000). His customer was the Ibaragi Prefecture Trucking Association, which planned to donate the material for use in a local pedestrian-safety campaign.

A fellow group general manager, Kiyoshi Murakami, had chosen June 23 to introduce for nationwide sale a new line of "Scotch" brand "Crystal" cassette tapes.

After the workday, Kenzo Tanabe and Harry A. Hammerly, president and senior managing director of the

Focusing on the future: A miniature 3M connector for electronic
components was pictured in many U.S. newspapers June 23. It reached Associated
Press Wirephoto subscribers by way of another 3M technology, laser beam
electronic transmission onto dry silver paper.

Daylight almost around the clock, for Trine Nordboe in Oslo.

Seminars, sales and safety products, saunas and song fests

company, respectively, gathered with a number of co-workers and customers for a 3M 75th anniversary party at the Tokyo American Club.

Service to schools and educators was on the agenda as other 3Mers met in Hong Kong that week.

They had gathered from eight 3M companies of Southeast Asia for a two-day training seminar on the features, advantages and benefits of visual products and overhead projection transparencies. Their hosts were Roger Lorenzini and Kenneth Yu of the Graphic Systems staff at 3M Far East Ltd. Seminar attendees came from as far as Manila on the east (Arthur Leoncio) to Bangkok on the west (Kitti Ariyapongse and Sunsun Kunnavatana).

While they studied, Richard Tsang was preparing a display booth for participation over the weekend in the Hong Kong Road Safety Association Exhibition for motorists. Some 20,000 interested consumers attended the event and many of them viewed Tsang's Victoria Park exhibit, which emphasized reflective license plates, helmets for cyclists, safety triangles and reflective fabric for the night-time safety of pedestrians and bicycle pedallers in the crowded Crown colony.

The business day expanded and the pace continued as June 23 dawned in the countries of Europe.

For Trine Lise Nordboe near the Arctic Circle in 3M Norway it was a long day, close to 19 hours from sunrise at 2:36 a.m. to sunset. With the company for six years, she had spent two years as hostess at the business machine demonstration center in Oslo and advanced to become a senior consultant and sales representative.

Before noon she had installed a new VHS (versatile, high speed) copier at *Aftenposten*, the largest newspaper in Norway. Part of her workday was spent in training the newspaper's personnel to use the machine properly. By late afternoon, she was able to practice her handball with other 3Mers and then relax in the employees' sauna facilities. ("Yes, the sauna is segregated, females only," she reported.)

Safety products on display in Victoria Park, Hong Kong.

It was a busy first week of summer. Earlier, as the elected employee representative on the board of 3M Norway, Trine had reviewed minutes of the last meeting and met with technical service personnel.

On Wednesday she conducted master operator training for Dyno Industries, a customer about to install a 12th copying machine. Then she lunched with a representative from the Royal Norwegian Air Force to discuss the possible installation there of a fifth VHS copier. A thick, black column of smoke gave her a scare as she returned to the office, but "I was happy to learn it came only from a test demonstration of 3M's 'Light Water' fire-fighting foam."

Thursday was Midsummer Eve, when "light spill" from the far north sun fills most of the night.

"I knew that most people leave their work early in the afternoon for the observance," Trine said later. "So I got up very early, and it paid. By lunch time I had obtained two renewals on office equipment contracts. Before seeing my last customer for the day—and being stuck in a traffic jam—I stopped in a shop to buy 100 picnic baskets for our Family Day outing for 3Mers and their families."

By the weekend, there was a welcome chill and rain in Oslo, which had been the hottest capital in Europe for several days.

Far to the south in Italy, on June 23, key account salesman Silvestro Romano was able to realize, with help from Gioacchino Pilotta, the sale of 14 office machine units in one order from the Interior Department in Rome.

One of their colleagues in 3M Italy, Loranzo Priorone, manager of training and education services, had assembled 20 of the company's marketing personnel for an intensive week of skill-sharpening.

It was a week of *bonhommie* and *gemutlichkeit* for other 3Mers elsewhere in Europe as they welcomed the vacationing, 47-voice 3M Male Chorus from Minnesota. Their June 23 concert at Cergy near Paris was the mid-point in a tour that had been planned and saved for through three previous years.

Other stops had taken them to Gorseinon, Wales, for a Jubilee Year concert and Beauchamp, France. Plant manager G. Denis Murphy noted that while all of the

A cafeteria concert for fellow 3Mers in Europe, and a trio of Welsh welcoming smiles for American chorus members.

United Kingdom was celebrating Queen Elizabeth's silver jubilee, more than 1,000 employees were also observing the 25th anniversary of 3M Gorseinon.

Final concerts of the trip were in Kamen, Westphalia, and Neuss, near Dusseldorf. Burgomeister Berg told 800 enthusiastic music fans at the Kamen Music Hall that he considered donation of all concert proceeds to the local Martin Luther King Workshop "a good symbol of the close relationship between the community and 3M."

Meanwhile, the crescendo of anniversary date activity within 3M had crossed the Atlantic to the Americas.

Brazilian John Godoy, chief engineer for 3M Brazil in the sprawling outskirts of Campinas, northwest of Sao Paulo, conferred with the company's Australian-born managing director David Brydon.

On June 23 they were discussing an interim report on the installation of a tape treater and maker, equipment which was urgently needed to fill customer needs in one of the fastest growing economies of South America.

Working on the project, during one of the warmest winters in Brazil's history, were George W. Nelson and Arthur P. Hutchinson, maintenance field service engineers from St. Paul, Minnesota. Their "field" is the world. Hutchinson spent a month on the job in Campinas and Nelson, a quarter-century 3Mer, was joined by his wife for part of his three-month field trip, which ended in July with the new equipment operational.

For technology sharing: awards to Gary King and George Drossos, on left, from Joe Kuhn and Bob Adams.

Five thousand miles north of Campinas, Canadian 3Mers Gary King, George Drossos and Dale Tucker were still receiving congratulations June 23 for awards given them two days earlier.

The three engineers, two in technical service and one in process engineering, had been among 90 some participants at an all day company technical seminar in a lecture room at Fanshawe College near 3M Canada's London, Ontario, headquarters. Technical directors in attendance had judged that papers presented by King, Drossos and Tucker were the best of the day.

On the scene from 3M Center, St. Paul, was Dr. Robert M. Adams, vice president, research and development, and a director of the parent 3M Company. He challenged the Canadian technical personnel to develop their own unique 3M products for worldwide sales. The challenge was repeated by Swiss-born Josef L. Kuhn, president and general manager of 3M Canada, expressing his own strong interest in seeing a significant product development program in Canada.

Roy Duxbury, 3M Canada's technical director, reported the seminar a success; through presentation of selected papers by their colleagues, laboratory personnel learned of the work and progress of others, a typically 3M kind of exposure, providing an opportunity to profit and learn from the problem-solving experiences of those in other divisions and countries.

By nightfall of June 23, many French Canadian 3Mers had joined their neighbors in celebrations that included folk music, bonfires and fireworks displays. It was the eve of St. Jean Baptiste Day and much of their festivity extended through the following day.

In the United States, where it all began 75 years earlier, tourist traffic along the north shore of Lake Superior was beginning to build up to its summer peak on Thursday, June 23.

A guest book at the Lake County Museum in Two Harbors, Minn., shows that more than 150 visitors from 14 U.S. states, Canada, England, Spain and Finland signed in and paused to view a newly installed display commemorating 3M's founding and early operations there and at Crystal Bay, several miles up the shore. By fall, close to 40,000 were expected to visit the museum, housed in a building which once served as a railroad depot.

Newspapers around the country that day took note of those long ago beginnings with articles about the "rocky, abrasive start" and the "wobbly infant" which stuck together for 75 years.

In 3M's headquarters community at St. Paul, the *Dispatch* editor printed birthday greetings to "a supplier of products which touch the lives of countless millions every day" with "the industrial answers to needs observed and anticipated." The company's "handsome spread of offices and plants" in Minnesota was called "a principal underpinning of the city's — and the state's and region's — economy. The 3M trademark, so ubiquitous and so instantly recognizable, is synonymous with industrial innovativeness and know-how and a badge of pride for a city and state which wish it the best on its 75th anniversary. The company looks upon 75 years as a fine beginning, and so do we all."

There were still new beginnings at 3M in mid-1977. Somewhere, spread through the operations were several dozen teams of entrepreneurial achievers aiming to earn a "Golden Step" award.

The award had been established by Raymond H. Herzog, chairman of the board and chief executive officer, to recognize those responsible for new business ventures which reach a specified level of sales and profitability. The significance of the award, given to a number of promising projects each year since 1973, is heightened for those who know that it took all of 3M more than 10 years to reach a similar stage of success and solvency in the early days of the century.

Achievement of another kind brightened the morning of June 23 for Charles R. Whitfield, operator of a slitter machine that makes smaller and narrower consumer-size rolls out of big ones in a 3M tape plant at Bristol, Pennsylvania. Only 20 months with the company, he had just set a plant production record with 225 cuts of filament tape during an eight-hour shift.

A new generation, half a mile from 3M Center, unaware of the role played by 3M pioneers A. G. Bush and W. L. McKnight. The streets were renamed in their honor in 1957.

THE GOLDEN STEP AWARD

1975 WINNERS

"Golden Step" team leaders from a single recent year.

Millions of yards daily of web-processed materials

On the morning of 3M's anniversary, he was telling Lewis W. Lehr, president, U.S. operations, how he does it. "I guess I did the talking," Whitfield recalls, "and Mr. Lehr did the listening. He really wanted to know about me and my job."

Lehr and James A. Thwaits, president, International operations, were in Pennsylvania that day with others, including Erwin W. Brown, vice president, manufacturing and Allen F. Jacobson, tape group vice president and a former Bristol plant manager. The chat with Whitfield was part of a series of plant visits that also took them to Bedford Park, Illinois, and to Thorofare and Freehold, New Jersey.

Whitfield's work that day made him part of a worldwide 3M team which produced on June 23 about 4 million square yards of web-processed materials, ranging from surgical drapes to printing plates.

To get a product where it's needed when it's needed — whether in a hospital, home, school, office or factory — required teamwork of others in sales branches and warehouses from Boston to Honolulu.

Al Breller, branch operations manager in Atlanta, Georgia, supervises the administrative and support force for one such team of close to 300 serving many of 3M's customers in a nine-state area from Key West to Knoxville, from Savannah to Vicksburg.

The night before June 23 Breller and Jack Palmer, branch sales manager for Industrial Abrasives, drove through a thunderstorm to Atlanta's airport to welcome a visiting group which included Walter S. Meyers, vice president, marketing, and Willis C. Rech, assistant treasurer and director of branch administration. The June 23 review of operations went well, recalls assistant branch operations manager Gene Nix, and mint juleps were in order.

Before the week was out, the same travelers had visited branch sales offices in Cleveland and Cincinnati, Ohio, and High Point, North Carolina.

They weren't the only 3M travelers. Another was Charlton Dietz, 46-year-old 3M board member and vice president, legal affairs. He began June 23 at a California meeting of the American Society of Corporate Secretaries and finished his workday at Duluth with other members of the Minnesota State Bar Association.

At one airport alone, Minneapolis-St. Paul International, 84 3Mers boarded planes on June 23 for flights to scientific meetings, on problem-solving missions to customers, or to inspect the work of an expansion project. It was an average day for the middle of the week. Weekend traffic of the same kind often climbs to 150 per day.

Inbound traffic includes suppliers and vendors, interested in helping 3M spend wisely its $6,700,000 in daily worldwide purchases.

June 23, 1977: Allen R. Dressler, a supervisor in 3M's environmental laboratory, missed his usual lunchtime run of six miles to Lake Phalen and back because 150 members of the American Society for Testing Materials wanted to hear about his methodology for wastewater testing . . . Personnel manager Sandy Bryant at Knoxville, Iowa, was conferring with Art Sidner, a St. Paul equal employment opportunity affairs supervisor, about the Iowa plant's plans to hire its first deaf employee . . . Richard L. Aspenson, manager of energy conservation, resources and planning, met with division manufacturing directors for an overview of 3M's energy programs . . . 40-year 3Mer John O. Elstad and his wife began their final packing for a move to Hilden, West Germany, and a new assignment as technical service manager for traffic control products in Europe. John's first visit to Germany came as a prisoner of war after his World War II photo-reconnaissance P-38 was shot down over Italy. "I'm looking forward to the trip," he winked. "This time I speak the language." . . . and Geri Burford, 27-year-old Webster, Wisconsin, native began her first day with 3M as a secretary in the Paper Products division at 3M Center in Minnesota.

Among the 83 reports, letters, invitations, requests, applications and other pieces of mail to reach the chairman and chief executive's office that day was a thoughtful summary of seminar proceedings from Bryn Mawr College.

Other commitments had kept 3M from attending the seminar on "Strengthening Communications Between the Concerned Shareholder and the Corporation." Excerpts from the seminar program and student reaction to it were passed along by Mary Patterson McPherson, acting president of Bryn Mawr.

Some at 3M were pleased to read her views about seminar participants having learned "that corporate executives are individuals with diversified interests and a keen awareness of the world about them." Students at the seminar also came to a better appreciation of the "awful lot of time and effort it takes to run a business" and to a realization "that corporations are managed by individuals

Charles Whitfield, right, telling Lew Lehr about his production record. Assistant personnel manager Jim White snapped the scene.

7

with the same hopes and goals as those who represent public interest groups."

In the summary of undergraduate comments, one noted the intricacy of the issues involved in corporate responsibility and the very delicate balance between competing or conflicting interests that a corporation must represent.

The conclusion had been that both corporations and activist shareholders are interested in developing bridges

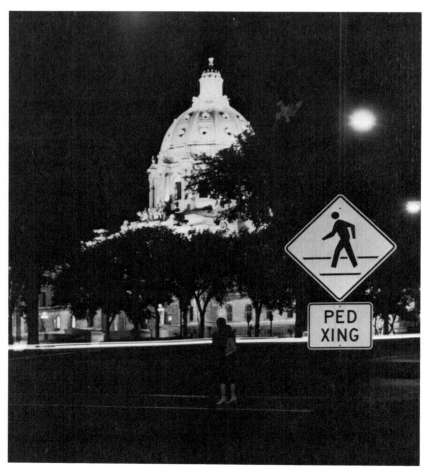

"Scotchlite" safety sign; capitol in background.

of communication and no single group has all the wisdom when it comes to making judgments or imposing particular value systems.

In Washington, D.C., that day there was business as usual. The senior U.S. Senator from Minnesota, Hubert H. Humphrey, took the time to insert a tribute to 3M in the *Congressional Record.* The *Record* for June 23 carries a brief entry, addressed to the Senate's presiding officer, Vice President Walter F. Mondale of Minnesota, and modestly headlined "The 3M Co. Is 75 Years Old":

"Mr. President, some 75 years ago, on June 23, 1902, articles of incorporation were filed for what has become a worldwide, diversified manufacturing organization of 80,000 people. I refer to Minnesota Mining and Manufacturing, commonly known as the 3M Co.

"A butcher, a doctor, a lawyer, and two railroad men were the five original incorporators of 3M at Two Harbors, Minn., on the north shore of Lake Superior in the center of North America. Their plans to mine a useful abrasive mineral never were realized. Consequently, the word "Mining" as part of the 3M name is a misnomer. But they turned to manufacturing, and their small firm grew by converting the needs of society into business opportunities.

"First it was a sandpaper, a pervasive tool of industry, to help smooth the world's rough edges. Then, Scotch brand tapes and adhesives to help hold an expanding world together. Today—through privately financed industrial research and development, through careful customer service, through quality control and truth in marketing—the list of 3M products and services has grown to include office systems and electrical products for better human communications, reflective signing for safer roads and bridges, new health care products for patient comfort, and packaging materials for fresher food—some 40 major product lines in all."

Humphrey's brief message continued:

"Too often in our interdependent civilization, we forget the relevance of sandpaper to pipes and plowshares, of tapes and other packaging materials to food and shelter, of all the behind-the-scenes technology that goes into the fabrication of wheels and wings and bridges to bring people together. Just as we tend to take for granted the marvels of magnetic recording tape—one of many 3M developments—we also tend to take for granted water at the push of the tap, light at the flick of switch, mobility at the turn of key, and a helpful human voice at the other end of a telephone line. As a trusted supplier of essential tools, materials, and equipment to others in industry and commerce, 3M is a partner in filling all of these and other categories of human need.

"On this anniversary of 3M Co.'s founding, I salute the people who have made possible such a fruitful, efficient, and productive socio-economic mechanism, mindful not only of the firm's good record as a taxpayer and of its thousands of industrious employees, but also of its more than 100,000 shareholders who reinvest some of each year's earnings, as seed money, in new and often risky ventures.

"From HHH to MMM, my friends and neighbors in Minnesota and elsewhere, I say Godspeed in pursuing your stated anniversary objective: to perpetuate the vitality of an organization which provides not only jobs and careers for many people, but also useful goods and services for others in society while exercising a prudent regard for all the resources entrusted to your use."

These remarks of a world-famous Senator, himself a former U.S. Vice President, provided welcome recognition from a powerful sector of society which claims close to one dollar out of every two earned by 3M.

Later, when all the entries for June 23, 1977, had been tallied, when all the pounds, yen, lire, pesos, francs, marks, kroner, dollars and other currencies had been counted, the controllers could report that worldwide sales for that single anniversary day had been $16,251,890, . . . greater than in any full year during the first half of 3M's 75-year existence and helpful in propelling 3M toward its first billion-dollar sales quarter, with more than $100 million in net earnings.

As usual, business on June 23 had been good enough to pay the bills, meet a payroll and have some funds left over for the next day's needs.

A sale here, a service there, a feeling of work well done. Some work and some play. All in all, not a bad day. ☐

We did, Jane Thomson; it was the 27,394th day in the life of 3M.

Dawn: A 3M Center scene from the '60s, when many new places to work took shape.

Building on a solid base

Years of vigor, growth and excitement were on the horizon

when 3M, once before, observed a birthday, its 50th

Many of us who have been with the Company nearly half its existence know that in some ways 3M has changed dramatically in the past three decades and in others hardly at all," says the 3M Annual Report for 1976.

"There is the same strong interest in research, quality, service and reliability. The same interest in knowing our customers, finding new markets, developing new businesses. The same reliance on people, individual initiative and personal responsibility."

Among the changes: a much larger role in filling needs on many new fronts.

"All of us recognize," Chairman Ray Herzog adds, "the important contributions made by William L. McKnight, our long-time president and board chairman, and all of the other early employees who performed well during 3M's formative years and helped shape what we believe to be a great company. They set an excellent example and provided a strong challenge for all who follow."

When 3M was 50 and the company paused to examine its roots and savor its heritage at the half-century mark, Herzog was only ten years into his business career: After forsaking a job as high school science teacher and coach, he had hired on as a quality control analyst in 3M's main abrasives plant.

By the anniversary year of 1952, he had become production manager for a litho plate project at a relatively new production plant, Chemolite, along the Mississippi river south of St. Paul. Still ahead of him was an assignment as project coordinator of an infant copying machine program and the challenge of building 3M's presence in the business equipment and office systems field.

The fanfare with which 3Mers celebrated their 50th anniversary had considerable justification. Their company was solvent and poised for more post-war growth. Their "Scotch" brand tape product line had in two short decades achieved world fame. The investment community was aware of the company's potential and 3M stock had split four for one just the year before.

With annual sales well past the $100 million mark and total employment surging beyond 10,000, even 3M's home town of St. Paul was beginning to pay more attention to the struggling firm, just off the East Seventh streetcar tracks, which had become affectionately known as "The Mining."

An anniversary book, commissioned at that time, makes no mention of Herzog.

In fact, *The Brand of the Tartan*, published in 1955, mentions none of the young workers who grew to assume the responsibility of guiding 3M in its 75th anniversary year. Some of them were still in school. One was an engineer in 3M's tape customer service laboratory, experimenting on the side to adapt 3M technologies for hospital use. Another was pioneering the production facilities for a new 3M company in Canada. The book of the '50s gave little hint of what the next quarter century was to bring. An ambitious press run of 25,000 was ordered for that story of 3M's early years. Within a decade, the company's payroll swelled to include numbers of people well beyond that figure; and the book was out of print and out of date. Copies survive, as a detailed record of two-thirds of 3M's *chronological* life. But its pages reflect less than a tenth of the reality of 3M in its 75th year.

Still on the horizon were developments that would bring instant replays into the world's living rooms with videotape, advanced office systems to the world of commerce, new patient care and diagnostic aids for medicine, and sophisticated electronic support for a shrinking world with four billion people.

By 1959, 3M was to become a contributor to U.S. space exploration. And ten years later, on July 20, 1969, 3M products were on the scene in more than a half dozen supporting ways when man first stepped on the moon.

There was no way chroniclers in the early 1950s could know that 3M's most exciting years were yet to come. But the stage had been set, partially by organizational changes announced in 1948.

Prior to that time, all of the company's executives were participating in the development and sale of each individual product, with the result that responsibility for profits was widely dispersed throughout the entire organization.

Efficient management under the traditional pyramid organization that had served a smaller 3M well was no longer possible. 3M was running the danger of slowly strangling on its own growth.

As an experiment four years previously, McKnight had formed an Adhesives division. At its top, he named a general manager with full authority and responsibility for its operation. A Roofing Granules division was established on the same basis.

"This move represents a departure from organization plans," he wrote then. "The overlapping in the use of facilities and services . . . has been forcing us to operate under a combination of horizontal and vertical management."

McKnight outlined new management rules for the Adhesives division. His remarks became the cornerstone of 3M organization.

"As our business grows," he pointed out, "it becomes increasingly necessary to delegate responsibility and to encourage men and women to exercise their initiative. This requires considerable tolerance.

"Those men and women to whom we delegate authority and responsibility, if they are good people, are going to want to do their jobs in their own way. These are characteristics we want and should be encouraged as long as their way conforms to our general pattern of operation.

"Mistakes will be made, but if a person is essentially right, the mistakes he or she makes are not as serious in the long run as the mistakes management will make if it is dictatorial and undertakes to tell those under its authority exactly how they must do their job.

"Management that is destructively critical when mistakes are made kills initiative and it's essential that we have many people with initiative if we're to continue to grow."

McKnight's experiment worked well. The company was reorganized in 1948 on a vertical basis. Five more divisions in addition to Roofing Granules and Adhesives were created: Coated Abrasives, Pressure-Sensitive Tapes, Reflective Products, Color and Chemical, and Electrical Insulation and Sound-Recording Tapes.

Each had its own vice president or general manager, sales force, production team and research laboratory.

With this type of structure, new divisions could be created as necessary without greatly increasing the burden on top management.

However, as the number of divisions increased, it became impractical to have the heads of all divisions report directly to the president. The solution: cluster divisions with related products and markets into product groups, each headed by a corporate vice president reporting to the president.

The first to head product groups were Bert S. Cross, Clarence B. Sampair and Joseph C. Duke. Cecil C. March, Robert L. Westbee and Robert W. Mueller were the next group vice presidents to be named.

"Over the years, we've discovered that when a division reaches a certain size, it has a tendency to spend too much of its time on established products and markets and a lesser amount on new products and businesses," says Herzog.

"When we break out these new businesses we appoint a new management team. We give people an opportunity to identify with a new business and become more important to 3M; and we find, almost without exception, that the new division begins growing at a faster rate. We also stimulate the established division to find other new products and markets which will help it meet our growth objectives."

Products have become departments, departments have become divisions and divisions have become groups. Examples include electrical and sound-recording tapes, two separate businesses which were combined in the late 1940s to form a division.

Plastic electrical tapes were soon joined by a wide variety of other products for the electrical industry, becoming first a single division and subsequently the several divisions which eventually became the Electrical Products group.

Similarly, magnetic tape's product line grew to include instrumentation tape and video recording tape, spawning several of the divisions which were later combined in a Recording Materials group. The development of printing products and copying systems led to what became two groups.

While 3M's growth has for the most part been internally generated, acquisitions have also played a role. The company's acquisitions policy was well stated by former Chairman Harry Heltzer when he said, "Not everything can be invented here, no matter how much we provide in the way of talent, imagination and dollars. Sometimes an acquisition is the obvious answer.

"We try to look carefully at the 'fit' between 3M and a potential acquisition, based on the contributions that will be made by both partners. Hopefully, there will be the kind of synergism that makes two and two equal five—or more. An acquisition may enable the company to get into a growth market quicker than we could if we developed the necessary products, manufacturing capability or sales

Early-day entrepreneurs in electrical products businesses:
W. W. Wetzel, R. V. Holton, R. L. Westbee.

Big Board status: McKnight and John L. Connolly,
long-time 3M legal counsel, with ticker tape recording first
trade of company shares at New York Stock Exchange in 1946.

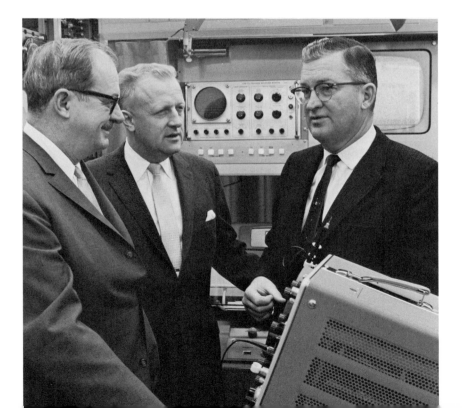

force ourselves. Sometimes, an acquisition merely enables us to fill out an existing product line."

Acquisitions played a role, for example, in the building of a Health Care Products and Services group, established in January 1972. Until that time the effort had been nurtured under the wing of the Tape and Allied Products group, where 3M medical products had their origins in an unsuccessful (and later perfected) surgical drape program of the early 1950s.

By 1970, 3M had a well-established Medical Products division and an expanding line of products for the health care field. One of them, "Micropore" tape, had been hailed as early as 1961 in a *Reader's Digest* article as the world's first "Adhesive Tape Without the Ouch!"

Other products in the line were finding worldwide uses, such as the "Aseptex" surgical mask used in Dr. Christian Barnard's headline-making, human heart transplant work. Dr. Barnard knew about 3M and the quality of its research from contact with lab workers while he was an obscure graduate student in surgery at the University of Minnesota.

Biochemical researchers at 3M had also been investigating pharmaceuticals for ten years. But 3M had neither the production facilities nor the sales force to make and market pharmaceutical products. The acquisition of Riker Laboratories provided a blend with 3M's own activities for an orderly expansion of health industry participation.

Robert W. Mueller, vice president in charge of medical as well as tape operations at the time of the Riker acquisition, noted "We acquired this fine company because of its sound management philosophy and experience in pharmaceuticals, its profitable operations and optimistic view of the future, its good reputation in the ethical drug industry and with the federal drug administration, and its international marketing strengths."

Acquisition of Dynacolor Corp. in 1963 and Ferrania S.p.A. the following year had played a similar role in the development of a Photographic Products division.

Bing Crosby, center, with 3Mer C. A. Kuhrmeyer and wife at Pebble Beach, California. The singer's Pro-Am Golf Tournament each January has been seen by national TV audiences under 3M sponsorship. 3M has also supported the charities which receive tournament proceeds.

Here again, the acquired companies brought technologies and products which complemented 3M's existing expertise and product lines.

Supplementing 3M's own plants, technologies and marketing strengths in such a way has often paid special dividends. New men and women of talent were integrated as well, and many of them thrived in their 3M environment, growing into new areas of division and corporate responsibility.

During a management meeting in 1957, 3M's chief executive officer was asked, "Just how big does 3M want to be?"

"Size," he replied, "is not so much an objective as it is a result.

"In my opinion, we will continue to grow in direct proportion to the ambitions of people who want a better future, both for themselves and for others whose condition can be improved through 3M products, services and know-how. To do less than our best at solving problems and filling needs would limit our growth, but I don't believe any of us want that."

The vertical organization concept, spelled out in 1948 to give each 3M division or subsidiary a measure of autonomy, did not extend to staff services. In many important ways, 3M remained a single integrated and interrelated business organization. As Herbert P. Buetow, president from 1953 to 1963, explained it, "We tried to maintain a balance between staff and operating management because we felt that the more highly specialized services can be administered more effectively at the staff level.

"Some companies carry the vertical organization to the extreme by putting all staff services such as engineering, legal, purchasing, accounting, public relations, personnel and others under divisional control. Our staff services have been continued on a centralized basis."

The growing sophistication and competence of staff functions provide an umbrella of support, and often the glue that holds a family of diverse, burgeoning businesses together.

Mapping the market for new business products:
E. F. Bovermann, left, and R. H. Herzog in the 1950s.

Cecil March, Hans Wessel and Joseph Duke at early 1950s groundbreaking for No. 6 Maker, world's largest sandpaper plant.

Financial expertise, for example, is one reason why 3M has often been cited as one of the best-managed companies in the U.S. Buetow, McKnight and other officers with a keen understanding of finance provided leadership in this area for many years. Their success is evident in the fact that, except for the period immediately following World War II, 3M was able to generate sufficient cash internally to meet its expansion needs for many years.

And when the company did seek outside financing during the recession of 1975, its excellent financial record earned 3M securities a triple-A rating. Fiscal controls, as practiced at 3M, have won admiring comment from many a visiting financial analyst.

Management guidelines require that a controller and an engineer, from corporate staffs, serve as assigned members on the management operating committee of each division. Results ideally include, in the case of engineering, a sharing of production know-how and processes and, in accounting, a constant, sensitive fingertip on the pulse of each operating unit, measuring progress and comparing performance with projections.

Senior management has encouraged a similar role for other staff services, so that the operating innovations and efficiencies of any single division can flow throughout the company.

As global inflation threatened world economies in the 1970s, a 3Mer with experience in international accounting and as a 3M managing director in inflation-troubled Brazil, Manuel J. Monteiro, was called on to tell other 3M managers what he had learned about "doing business in an inflationary economy."

Meanwhile, centralized staff groups were encouraged to develop expertise in depth, offering individual divisions the services of a specialist without the cost of having each division staffed for every contingency in an increasingly more complex business environment.

Patent affairs, government regulatory expertise, personnel and market research, public affairs, distribution and export services, purchasing—all grew to keep pace with the needs of 3M's multiplying businesses.

The small crew of purchasing agents under Beverly B.

Among the new beginnings: above, with indigenous "3M" cheerleaders and Gov. Mark Hatfield at Medford, Ore., in 1964; top, with six-guns, ten-gallon hats and Gov. John Connally at Brownwood, Texas, in 1966; left, with plant manager Al Moum and a scalpel to open the Brookings, S.D., medical products plant in 1971; and, top left, with imported snowballs and Winter Carnival royalty in southern California, 1973.

17

*Lynn Anderson in computer center where information
on 110,000 sales-related transactions at U.S. branches
is processed in 20 minutes nightly for use
in billings, customer analysis, inventory reports,
factory "make orders."*

Countryman, which had worked "miracles" in the materiel-short war years to keep abrasives and tape-production lines operating, became seven teams of specialists in the diverse commodities, supplies, equipment and services used by 3M.

It was a time when inkwells gave way to ball point pens. Computer printouts displaced ledger sheets. Inventory records could no longer be kept on the back of an envelope in an inside suit pocket as had happened in 3M's earliest years. DC-3s gave way to 600-mile-per-hour jets, and no part of 3M's farflung U.S. operations was more than two and a half hours from headquarters.

Worldwide elements of the company drew close as well with advances in communications services, many of them made possible by 3M's own technological contributions in computer tape, facsimile transmission, terminals, connectors and telephone cable splicing systems.

A technical magazine, *Communications News*, published a profile in 1972, examining the structure and operations of the 36-member communications department which at that time kept 3Mers in touch with each other and their customers.

Title of the illustrated article: "3M Develops Quality Communications System to Match Its Quality Products and People." It spoke with awe of the company's $20 million annual expenditure, amounting then to a penny out of every sales dollar earned, for this one staff service.

The telephone bill alone was more than $9 million in 1972 and those who maintained internal telephone directories were entering 800 changes a month as 3M and its people grew and progressed. Computerized message switching networks, data circuits, private wire systems and leased wires helped link more than 100 U.S. locations and about half as many overseas stations.

The small staff department's goal was simply stated by communications services manager James R. Jensen: "We want to expedite 3M message traffic, reduce 3M telephone and wire costs, and simplify 3M communications generally. All we want from 3M managers is their communications problems so that we can find solutions for them."

As elsewhere in the company, the aim was to stay fit and flexible. Change was constant.

A change toward greater integration of international and group marketing efforts took place in 1973.

The nine-member board of directors of the early 1950s had expanded to include a larger representation of outside talent. By the mid-1970s, there were 14 board members, including executives of several other firms and two former U.S. Cabinet members.

Other changes had seen Cross succeed Buetow as president in 1963 and then advance to become chairman of the board and chief executive officer when McKnight left the chairmanship in 1966.

Heltzer was elected president in 1966 and in turn advanced to become chairman and chief executive from 1970 to 1975. By November of 1975, when sales were at the $3 billion-a-year level and Herzog was serving as board chairman, chief executive and worldwide operational chief, directors agreed with the chairman in his stated conviction that leading 3M was more than a one-person job.

Two presidents were elected, Lewis W. Lehr for U.S. Operations and James A. Thwaits for International Operations. The tape lab worker who had experimented with surgical drapes in the early 1950s and the British-born engineer who was building 3M Canada in 1952 had new jobs, again.

Sales figures provide one inflation-flawed measure of 3M's continuing growth during the past three decades. But much of it was real growth. From $75 million in 1946 and $330 million in 1956, sales grew to $1.1 billion in 1966 and $3.5 billion in 1976.

"In Duluth in 1906, no one dreamed 3M would be a billion-dollar corporation," McKnight said at a supervisory-management meeting in commenting on 3M's first billion-dollar sales year in 1965. "Our problem then was just to stay in business."

The milestones began to occur faster. After 3M passed the $2 billion sales mark in 1972, Cross observed: "This convinces me that we have one of the finest organizations in the world. Reaching this level must have represented

Internal auditing team of three, Darrell Lindgren, Mary Morris and senior auditor Mary Fashingbauer at Distribution Center.

Annual stockholder meetings, then and now:
A small room held the crowd in 1950.
More than 4,000 have attended recent meetings.

Louis Anderson, right, of rubber compounding receives
first share of ownership under a new employee stock purchase plan from
John L. Connolly. At left is the plan's first administrator, Irwin R. Hansen.

"My middle initial is 'L' and that stands for land"

the best effort and teamwork of every man and woman in the employ of the company."

While employment grew, the 3M stockholder family also expanded from roughly 4,000 shareholders at the end of World War II to about 123,000 holders of more than 115,000,000 shares in the 75th anniversary year.

Listed since 1946 on the "Big Board" of the New York Stock Exchange, 3M also is traded at exchanges in Chicago, Los Angeles, Paris, Amsterdam, Switzerland and Germany. In August 1976, 3M was selected as a component of the 30-stock Dow Jones Industrial Average—perhaps the most widely watched barometer of American enterprise.

Stockholders have shared in 3M's success, collecting dividends without fail four times a year ever since the first 6-cent per share dividend was declared in 1916. They also benefited from their selection of directors through the years who used close to half of each year's after-tax earnings as seed money for expansion. The growth that resulted made 3M stock a fruitful investment for many, including employees. Under the first general employee stock option plan in 1950, for example, the share price was $97.20. That single share, as a result of four stock splits and appreciation in the intervening years, became 48 shares, worth $2,400 at mid-1977 market prices.

Cyril P. Pesek, an architect turned corporate engineering executive, recalls how some of the seed money was used.

"The division managers in the late 1940s and early '50s would give me their sales projections," says Pesek, "and I would translate them into bricks and mortar and equipment—and convert that into dollars. It was up to us to put together a story to present to the board of directors. In other words, here's what is necessary to meet these sales forecasts. It was up to the board to decide whether and where they wanted to spend the stockholders' money."

Pesek also recalls the beginnings of 3M Center, now grown in 3M's third quarter-century from a single building with 200 employees to a campus-like complex of a dozen major buildings and 10,000 employees.

"I remember when McKnight called me in and said, 'Cy, take a look around the whole Twin Cities metropolitan area to see if you can find a site on which we can build a central research laboratory and put other laboratories later.' We started on that project."

Pesek found a 30-acre site at the eastern edge of St. Paul, surrounded by pasture and corn fields. But McKnight had gazed again into his crystal ball.

"We're growing very rapidly," McKnight told Pesek. "How much research and administration space do we need for a billion-dollar company?"

The dream was examined and translated to square feet of office and laboratory space. And Pesek went back to buy the entire farm, a mile long and a half-mile wide. "Buy the whole thing," McKnight is quoted as saying, "my middle initial is 'L' and this means land; buy plenty of land." This lesson was learned well, and used as 3M factories expanded into outstate Minnesota, Wisconsin, Pennsylvania, New Jersey, Alabama, California and elsewhere.

To meet the research needs for generating 3M's future into the 21st century, a second research/office park

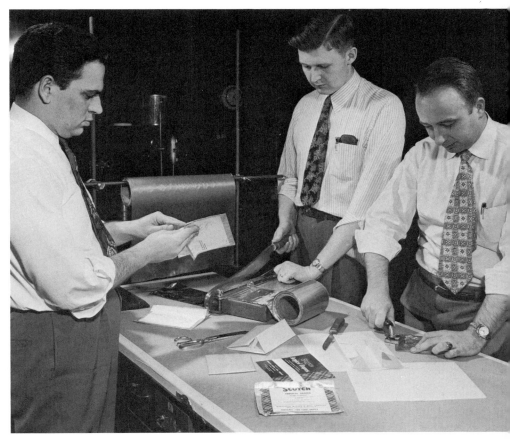

1950 pilot plant scene: B. Y. Auger, R. C. Bertelsen and L. W. Lehr work on surgical drape packaging.

dollars, long before it will be possible to place one stone upon another. Meanwhile, the 3M Center grounds-keeper began using the proposed expansion site to grow a new crop of trees for landscaping purposes.

At the end of World War II, 3M had plants in only three cities. By 1977, there were plants in 78 communities in 28 states. Physical growth in other parts of the country and the world was keeping pace.

The years brought problems and disappointments, as well. Perhaps the most serious and traumatic was a 1973 disclosure that corporate funds had been used to make illegal political contributions. People both inside and outside the company were shaken by the news, but the comments that meant the most—and hurt the most—were those from 3M employees. Some were written directly to top officers.

"As a member of the 3M family, I was hurt deeply and felt personally betrayed," wrote Lois S. Dorsey, a sales branch secretary, from her home in Baldwin Park, Calif., shortly after the wrongdoing was acknowledged by 3M to Watergate investigators in 1973.

"Some people have been surprised at my reaction. They have commented that lots of companies did the same thing, that politics are always 'dirty,' that no one person can change the system and that St. Paul is not interested in what I think.

"I disagree on all points. Because other companies have shown poor judgement does not excuse an illegality on the part of my company . . . I believe I *can* change the system by making my views known and by encouraging others, individually and corporately, to honest and dedicated service to politics . . . And finally, I disagree that St. Paul is uninterested in my thoughts on the subject. 3M stresses and expects integrity from its employees. It follows that employees may stress and expect integrity from 3M Company."

Her reaction was not unique.

"At the age of 45, I seldom find myself shocked or surprised by human failing," said Thomas B. Leivermann, manager of employee records, in another note handwritten to the chairman and chief executive officer.

Employee Clown Club members entertain at hospital for crippled children.

entered the planning stage in the mid-1970s. Located several miles northeast of 3M Center, the new site—named Carlton Park in honor of Richard P. Carlton, 3M president in 1949-53—is expected, according to initial projections, to provide work space for up to 18,000 additional employees when fully developed over a period of decades.

Years of elaborate environmental impact studies and zoning considerations had cost 3M more than a million

"Disclosure of 3M's involvement in illegal campaign financing is an exception. I would like to register my anger and humiliation at this serious breach of integrity. What happened to our pride and self-respect?"

Even before the dust had settled and the corporate funds had been replaced, an editorial in employee publications offered the view that "many of us feel hurt and disappointed. But at times, we may have to remind ourselves that people, even good people, make mistakes." Steps were taken to avoid a recurrence.

Some of the mistakes, failings and failures at 3M have been easier to live with, however.

"Management's attitude toward new product development should be one that permits learning to live with a lot of failures, because they are inevitable," says Lehr. "It takes a bit of resiliency to bounce back after the first failure, a little bit more on the second, and it takes a pretty durable and flexible management to keep its equilibrium after the ninth and tenth failures.

"It is mighty easy to get discouraged and it takes a special brand of person to weather all the storms.

"Some one person must have the courage, the resiliency, and the determination to stick with the thing through its growing pains, sell his ideas to others, and in the end, to reap a handsome reward in both dollars and personal accomplishment. It seems also that each of these revolutionary developments opens the door for a whole chain of other new product ideas, filling more needs and leading to a whole series of new businesses.

"At 3M we look to new product development to help us continue to diversify our product line and to sustain and nourish our long term growth potential. There is no magic formula involved—it just takes men and women with ideas who are not afraid of work. We think that's the kind we have at 3M."

"Of course, in the process of growing and diversifying, along with some outstanding successes, we've had some resounding flops," Lehr adds. "The secret, if there is one, is to dump the flops as soon as they are recognized, and get back to something that is profitable. But even the flops are valuable in certain ways. As someone once said: you can learn from success, but you have to work at it; it's a lot easier to learn from a failure."

As 3M research and production facilities grew, strong marketing teams continued traditions of customer service and satisfaction, with roots deep in the company's past. It came as no great surprise, though a welcome form of recognition, when *Forbes* magazine called the company's marketing team "one of the great, truly flexible marketing organizations in the capitalist world."

The 3M marketing philosophy was stated well by former marketing vice president John F. Whitcomb in these words:

"Ralph Waldo Emerson is supposed to have said: 'Build a better mousetrap and the world will make a beaten path to your door.' Well, Emerson may have been one of the

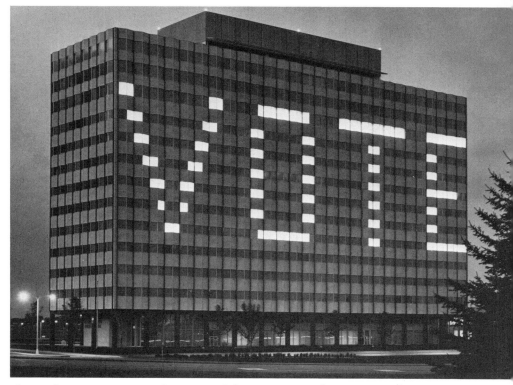

The medium was very much a part of the message in this 3M appeal to citizens just before the 1964 U.S. presidential election. The Christian Science Monitor *and other newspapers front-paged the picture across the land.*

most influential figures of the nineteenth century, but he didn't know beans about beaten paths. If you wait for the world to beat a path to your door, you very likely will end up with a warehouse full of mousetraps. The point is, better mousetraps won't *bring* people to your door—you have to go out and sell them.

"This is true whether the product is a new idea, a new application of an existing product, or a variation on it. And it is important that 3M continue to bring to the market all three. As one manufacturer puts it:

"The future will belong not to the business with best facilities, or products, or technologies, or even the best people—important as those factors are. The future will belong to those entrepreneurs who best sense the wants and needs of potential customers, and then marshal people, facilities and technologies to serve them."

Just as technologies were blended for synergistic service to new markets and processes were shared for manufacturing efficiencies, a corporate advertising program evolved to support the overall marketing effort and enhance 3M's image, and a grapevine-system of sharing sales leads developed among the members of different 3M sales forces.

Packaging guidelines and a corporate identification program of the 1960s made the blue 3M logo a familiar sight at receiving docks of firms in virtually every industry.

For a number of years in the 1960s, some of the U.S. corporate advertising took the form of television documentary sponsorship. Both the commercial messages and the programming won awards—among them an Emmy award for excellence in public interest television and a Lasker Award for outstanding medical journalism. A print of one program on the early days of flight, "From Kitty Hawk to Paris," was donated in 3M's 75th anniversary year to a museum in Charles A. Lindbergh's hometown, on the 50th anniversary of his solo, trans-Atlantic flight.

By the mid-1970s, 3M's television programming efforts had shifted to the underwriting of special programs for Public Broadcasting Service (PBS).

The new PBS programs addressed concerns of society such as the problems of the aged, alcoholism, venereal disease, learning disabilities among children, and breast cancer. People in need were stimulated by the programs to take a step toward seeking help, and 3M made the help more accessible through incentive grants to local PBS stations. The objective of the grants: to encourage as many stations as possible to follow up the national programs with local information, providing viewers with answers to phoned-in questions and guidance on obtaining help. People with problems responded. This "Community Outreach" approach resulted in more than 100,000 viewer inquiries from each of the PBS programs. A newspaper editorial described the program as "one of the best examples of corporate recognition of social responsibility we've seen in a long time."

Robert H. Tucker, when serving as first chairman of a board of directors committee on corporate responsibility, advanced a broader view: "Corporate responsibility is more than frosting on the cake. It must be part of everything we do at 3M. But, because we have a healthy

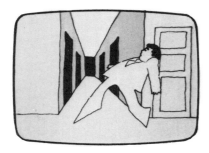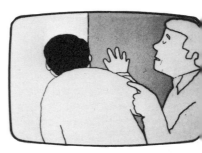

"Chameleon Man" shyly blends into file cabinets and water cooler until his ideas are sought by 3M co-workers. The 1971 TV commercial won awards: Lion d'Or prize at Cannes, and "best animation" and "best corporate commercial" honors in the U.S.

business, our combined talents and resources as a corporation permit us to reach out and help society in additional ways that most individual persons could not afford."

He and others were always quick to add that the company's first responsibility is to perform its major economic role well — that is, to harness resources in a productive and profitable way. Having done this, the company is then in a position to make other socially desirable contributions.

In a typical year, grants to educational institutions account for about half of 3M's philanthropic contributions. Civic organizations, medical missionaries, and cultural groups share in the balance. Private college funds in some 30 of the United States are regular recipients of 3M grants, as is the United Negro College Fund.

Forty children of employees are selected each year, on the basis of National Merit test scores, to receive four-year college scholarships.

"Scholarships are a financial help," wrote John Lupo of the Printing Products division in appreciation. His doctor daughter's medical education had been made possible in part by a 3M National Merit Scholarship. "But equally important," Lupo wrote, "is the sense of accomplishment that this recognition instills in young people at an early, important stage of their lives. It lets them know that the extra effort was worth it."

One form of aid to education was expanded during 3M's 75th anniversary year at the prompting of a retired employee.

An earlier plan whereby employees can make gifts to

No stone unturned

At a meeting in the U.S. Treasury Department, in the early fifties, a trio of 3Mers found they could leave no stone unturned — or unidentified.

Jack Brown, 3M geologist, John Connolly, general counsel, and Bob Tucker, a young attorney, were meeting with the Treasury's chief geologist to discuss a ruling relating to industrial minerals.

The federal geologist, described by Tucker as "an old curmudgeon," wasn't convinced that these midwesterners knew enough about geology to be taking up his time. Gesturing to some rocks in his office, he growled: "I'm going to pick out three rocks. If you can identify two out of three, I'll give you a passing grade and may listen to you. If you get all three, I'll believe what you're telling me."

Connolly and Tucker quickly agreed before consulting Brown, who went on trial without, as he said later, "benefit of counsel." Brown took the first sample with trepidation and examined it: "That's almandite garnet from around North Creek, N.Y."

The second was a gray rock. Brown inspected it carefully before identifying it as North Carolina granite. "Right on the nose," Tucker recalls and the stern "judge" raised an eyebrow.

Then came the moment of truth. The Treasury geologist reached into his desk and brought forth a chamois-skin bag that contained a piece of jewel-like obsidian material. "I'm no precious-gem expert," objected the perspiring Brown, but his protests got no sympathy.

Brown nervously examined the mineral, hefting it first in one hand, then the other. He tasted it, smelled it, scratched it and pinched it. "Finally, after what seemed like an eternity," Tucker recalls, Brown spoke: "If this isn't a precious stone," he said, "then it is natural-tar rock, probably from the Lake Athabasca region."

Brown had scored again — three out of three. The federal geologist was visibly impressed, Tucker remembers, "and from that point on gave us respect and the 3M matter careful attention."

Following the meeting, a libation seemed in order, a motion which even the teetotaling Connolly seconded. "I'll take anything," Brown told the waiter, "as long as it's not on the rocks."

Classroom students as well as congressmen and business leaders heard Chairman Heltzer in the 1970s, sharing 3M views on the role of world trade and multinational firms.

eligible educational institutions and have their donations matched, dollar for dollar, by the 3M Foundation had been well received. Retiree Ken Keim had an idea. During a question and answer period at 3M's annual stockholder meeting in May 1977, he took the floor amidst a crowd of more than 3,000 to ask whether 3M would consider extending the "matching grant" opportunity to retirees. He was promised prompt consideration for his suggestion.

Keim soon had an answer. Yes. The company had decided to match the educational gifts of pensioners who retired directly from 3M on the same terms as it matched donations by current employees. And the yearly maximum per individual to be matched was increased from $1,000 to $1,500.

In uncounted ways and sometimes in untallied dollar amounts, the response by 3M and its people has often been "yes," whether the appeal was for disaster aid abroad or United Way support at home in any of the scores of communities that 3M calls home.

"We are satisfied that 3M is moving in the right direction on most of the concerns expressed by our employees, the public and government," says Dr. R. M. Adams, successor to Tucker as chairman of the board committee on corporate responsibility. "We don't always agree at first among ourselves as to the proper interpretation of the need or the best solution. However, we are convinced that there are good 3M people involved in all these areas, that they are sensitive to the issues and will find solutions to problems we face."

The areas referred to include human relations, equal opportunity programs, consumer affairs and customer relations, truth in advertising, worker health and safety, resource conservation and respect for the environment — none of them new concerns at 3M but some of them newly articulated as others in society displayed increasing awareness and the company itself assumed a larger role and profile in the world.

As 3M chief in 1948, McKnight spoke out on resource conversation in words that read well three decades later, even after a series of energy crises.

He wrote, as an industrialist, in a conservation

publication. After acknowledging 3M's humble heritage from an earlier era when the company had no choice but to avoid waste and conserve resources if it was to survive, he observed, writing in the late 1940s:

"It's only in recent years that conservation of natural resources has become of interest to people generally. Even now, there are too few who consider conservation a major part of business operations; but the number is growing and for that the nation should be grateful."

McKnight was both perceptive and plain-spoken:

"Too often we think of conservation as pertaining only to wildlife, fish and our forests. The term means a great deal more than that."

He went on to mention specifically the pending threat of a fossil fuel shortage, adding:

"In industry, almost any saving of materials is at least an indirect saving of our natural resources and manufacturers who recognize this are probably operating at a much higher level of efficiency than those who do not. That efficiency, through more thorough use of materials, means more economical production. That in turn means more total production for each invested dollar, . . . more jobs, more prosperity."

For the most part, his kind of thinking has prevailed within 3M. For example:

• One of the first persons with a doctorate in sanitary engineering was working at 3M more than a decade before the initial "Earth Day" observance in 1970 focused popular attention on the environment.

• 3M in 1976 was the first industrial firm to receive a U.S. Federal Energy Agency citation for its conservation programs.

• Innovative 3Mers are continually invited to address technical and governmental sessions on various pollution control and prevention programs, on 3M's internal energy conservation guidelines, or on a 3M-pioneered program to employ 12-passenger vans instead of individual cars for the mass movement of commuting workers.

One frequent spokesman at congressional hearings, United Nations programs, industry conferences and other meetings has been Dr. Joseph T. Ling, 3M vice

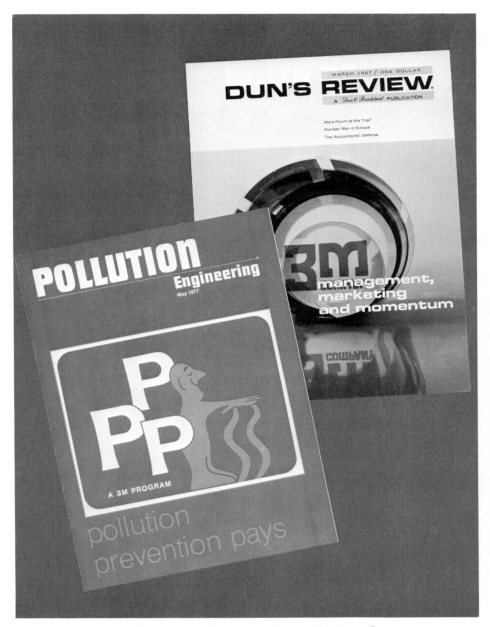

Magazine cover articles, among those of the '60s and '70s, reflect two views outsiders found newsworthy about 3M.

president for environmental engineering and pollution control. He has been frank and realistic in pointing out that while environmental issues are *emotional* and environmental decisions are *political*, the environmental solutions are *technical*.

Ling has also been known to trade on his Chinese origins, while avoiding confrontation tactics and adversary positions.

Discussing a "Pollution Prevention Pays" program, Ling noted that it was developed at 3M to reduce or eliminate pollution at the source rather than using an energy-inefficient and often counter-productive clean-up device at the end of a process. Referring to the latter method as a "black box" approach, he jokingly calls on an oft-quoted Oriental philosopher: "Confucius say, this is costly as hell."

While calling for greater industry-government cooperation and expressing wonder over the sometimes conflicting regulatory requirements and demands from society, Ling asked the "inscrutable Occidentals" in one audience, including some from the Carter administration: "Have *you* ever tried to eat peanuts with chopsticks?"

It *sounds* difficult.

In the business climate of the '70s, many at 3M would agree that issues are emotional and decisions are often political. They might even agree with Ling that environmental solutions often *are* technical.

For most of its solutions, however, 3M continues to look to people. But even then there is a case to be made for chemistry among people . . . and peoples.

"An organization does not flourish only by virtue of the superior talents it enlists," said Lyle H. Fisher, 3M personnel executive for 30 years. "All business organizations fish in the same pool and it is unlikely that any one net catches fish better than any other net.

"Our advancement will stem from providing for our people a better climate for achievement — a climate which stimulates ordinary people to produce extraordinary performances. The extent to which any one of us can produce beyond his or her rated capacity may be small indeed, yet the sum of these, when added together, will make the difference between a great organization and an indifferent one." ◻

From maker to market: jumbo jets play a part in export operations

Chemistry among peoples: First meeting of managing directors in the summer of 1955 brings together 3M executives from France, Germany, Canada, Brazil, Mexico, Australia and England.

A long way from Crystal Bay

A wallboard partition, riddled from the other side with peepholes, was all that separated the 3M France plant from that of a competitor when Werner Herold started the French company.

A. R. Fredriksen lived in a partially bombed out building when he was assigned to help 3M Germany build up its production of "Scotchlite" reflective sheeting.

Ramesh Shah started with 3M Kenya as financial manager but he also had to hand-deliver the first order to the first customer.

Oscar Orantes Troccoli was one of four sales people sharing a three-person office in Guatemala City—as a result they had to arrange travel schedules so they never all would be in the office at the same time.

3M France was established in 1951 and Werner Herold served as its managing director for 15 years, then became a vice president in 3M's European management. It was three years after the start of the French company that Norwegian-born Fredriksen went to 3M Germany from the United States. After a long career in International, Fredriksen became vice president of the Health Care Products and Services Group in 1975. It was 1970 when Shah, who became general manager of 3M Kenya and later managing director, joined that company. And it was two years after that when Orantes, later a group manager of the 3M Guatemala Division of 3M Interamerica, Inc., was playing musical chairs with his colleagues in Central America.

The humble beginnings tell much about 3M's International Operations. Indeed, humble beginnings are still happening. 3M continues to expand into new territories—to establish operations in countries that have a good potential for sales of 3M products.

There is a major difference between the 1970s and the

Some 3M pressure-sensitive tape was slit at a small Durex plant in Brazil in the late 1940s.

International operations were in their infancy when orchestra leader Guy Lombardo, center, helped McKnight, left, Bush and others observe 3M's 50th anniversary in 1952.

Magnetic tape slitting is a precision operation in the 1970s at 3M United Kingdom's plant in Gorseinon, Wales.

Growing globally—the 3M way—has produced customers, co-workers and friends on six continents

International Operations president James A. Thwaits, left, and 3M executive Manuel J. Monteiro, with officials of 3M Italy at a management meeting.

1950s, however. When 3M launched its International operations, the first companies were organized primarily in industrialized countries. In the 1970s, the expansion also has been taking place in the developing, or Third World, nations.

Two different worlds. In the first, the industrialized, 3M found cultures and needs similar to those in the United States. In the developing countries, the attitudes, the outlook, the way of life, the needs are profoundly different. A labor-saving product is welcome in a high employment country but not in one where 25 percent or more of the labor force is without work.

Yet, some of the same formulas have been used.

No matter in which country 3M operates—the United States or any other—it has started small and gradually built up its facilities and its number of employees as its sales volume warranted. 3M has gone into business in various countries with the intent to stay—to provide not just jobs but career opportunities for its employees in every country, to serve customers' needs on a continuing

basis and to open new markets for 3M products and technologies.

This meant 3M needed to build operations with potential for long-term growth. From its experience in the United States, the company found that such growth could best be achieved by establishing companies that were self-generating and by expansions that were self-financed.

For example, from an investment of $6.9 million by the parent company, 3M Germany's assets in 25 years of operation grew to $126 million, with those assets helping provide jobs for about 3,100 people.

As in the parent company, half of earnings after taxes are reinvested in the business in each country.

Ultimately, the responsibility for building up those assets falls to individuals like Shah and Orantes.

"We pin the rose of responsibility on the managing director of each company," said James A. Thwaits, president of International Operations. He credits this philosophy to his predecessors — Clarence B. Sampair, president of the original International division from 1952 to 1965, and Maynard H. Patterson, general manager and later group vice president, International, from 1956 to 1971.

The 3M companies in the International operations—most of them wholly owned subsidiaries but a few joint ventures—are autonomous legal entities that operate with a great deal of independence under general guidelines from corporate management. As principal stockholder, the parent company has majority representation on the board of directors of each wholly owned subsidiary.

The formulas have worked well. 3M's International Operations in 46 countries in 1976 accounted for approximately 40 percent of the company's sales or more than 3M's entire business nine years earlier.

Clarence B. Sampair, "father" of International, listens to presentations at 1970 annual meeting in St. Paul.

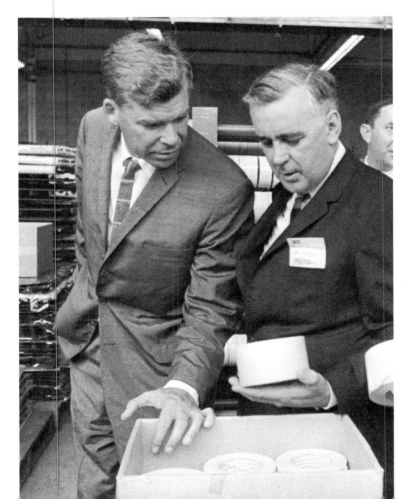

Maynard H. Patterson, right,
tours 3M Australia plant in 1964. With him, Bruce E. Chapman,
later managing director of that company.

International sales had grown from less than $20 million in 1951, the first year of 3M's direct entry into international markets, to 1.4 billion in 1976.

Moreover, at the end of that year, those operations were providing jobs for 34,000 people in the countries where they were located and another 6,500 jobs in the United States that are directly and indirectly dependent on the company's international business—from making products for export to providing staff support to the International companies.

Obviously, the modest beginnings have led to some substantial operations, paralleling the U.S. operations in diversity and complexity if not in total size. 3M France in 1977 became the fourth of 3M's largest manufacturing companies to move into newly completed office buildings in the decade. The 14-level French structure houses 1,000 people with room for expansion. In addition, 3M France has plants in two locations that manufacture abrasives, adhesives, pressure-sensitive tapes, "Scotch-Brite" products, copying paper, medical products and electrical products.

A product group manager in one of 3M's larger International companies may be responsible for a business the size of one of the parent company's product divisions. On the other hand, a sales representative in one of 3M's smaller companies may have to sell unrelated products from five or six divisions because his markets aren't big enough and his company hasn't been in business long enough to be more specialized. That will come with time.

3M's International operations are full of such contrasts. Although most 3M managers in each country speak English, some 20 major languages are spoken in the 40-plus countries where 3M operates. Those operations are on six continents in virtually every time zone. Often a 3Mer in one part of the world has awakened in the middle of the night to phone a colleague in another part of the world to help complete an important sale.

In mid-1977, the non-U.S. companies ranged in size from that of P. T. 3M Indonesia with 23 employees to 3M Italy with 5,250 employees. Actually, the smallest was 3M Ecuador, which was starting out on July 1 with one employee—its general manager, Jose I. Carreras.

Twenty-nine of the companies had manufacturing operations—from converting semi-finished goods to making a product from raw materials. Some had several plants in two or more locations; others slit tape or assembled copying machines in a corner of a warehouse.

Some 900 people were employed in laboratory facilities in 26 countries, doing work ranging from quality control and technical service to product modification and, increasingly, to product development.

Product research and development—as opposed to product modifications—outside the United States primarily have been done only at Minnesota 3M Research Limited in Harlow, England, and at 3M Italy's Photographic Laboratory. The former is a corporate research facility established in 1961 to specialize in photographic research but has since expanded into other product lines. 3M Italy's laboratory had its beginnings in the acquisition by 3M in 1964 of Italy's largest photographic manufac-

Thwaits, center, shares a farewell moment with E. C. Woods, managing director of 3M South Africa, and Mrs. Woods when Thwaits left an International area job in 1972 to head Tape and Allied Products group.

turer, Ferrania, S.p.A. Ferrania was merged with 3M Italy in 1971.

In 1977, two electrical products research facilities were launched in Japan and Germany with the objective of developing new technologies as well as adapting products. The Japanese facility is an expansion of Sumitomo 3M's Electrical Products laboratory aimed at serving the market in that part of the world. The German laboratory is set up as a separate company with a multinational staff that aims to develop products for countries which follow what is called the European electrical standard.

Like 3M in the United States, each of the International companies sells a broad range of products. Not all companies sell all products from every corporate division—but they would if they could. Sometimes there isn't the demand, or sometimes the company doesn't yet have the resources to hire and train the sales and technical service people needed to serve customers adequately with a particular product.

Who decides what is going to be sold in each country? The local management—and not just the managing director. Rather, the managing director acting on the recommendations of sales and marketing managers who are in most cases nationals of the country who know the market well, know what the market demands, and know how to sell in it. Whoever heard of promoting "Scotch" brand retail adhesives at a bicycle race in the United States? But that's what they've done with great success in France.

"I don't expect the International companies to be stamped out of the same cookie cutter as 3M U.S.," says International president Thwaits. "Certainly, we want close communications between the U.S. and International operations, but we have no right to stifle the creativity and initiative of people in other countries. They have their own goals and ambitions.

"We give our people in other countries guidelines and tell them certain things they are not allowed to do, but we try to keep that to a minimum. We can tell them the way we are doing things in the United States and why we are doing them that way, but we don't tell them they have to do the same things."

Bernard Lee, specialist in dye chemistry, works with distillation unit in Harlow, England, laboratory experiment.

*In Spain,
"Scotch-Brite" becomes
"The magic, green
American fiber."*

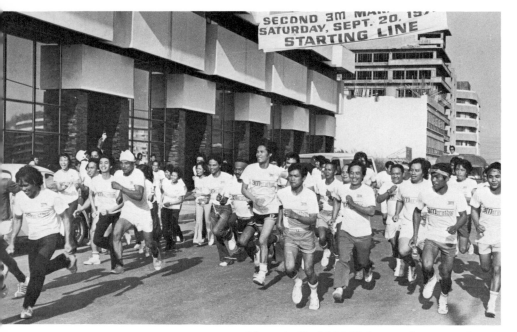

*About half of 3M Philippines' 400 employees
run in annual company marathon.*

3M Italy's startup "taught everybody that we do have muscle...if we all pull together"

Yet, despite the differences, there are certain common characteristics.

"There's a thread of intensity no matter where you go in the company," said Frank C. Zoccola in 1974, when he was director of international marketing for abrasives.

"We talk basically the same language and we are working toward the same objectives," said Magne Roetnes, a group cost accountant of 3M Norway, when he visited St. Paul in 1977 to learn more about how the headquarters operates.

And very early in the game, 3M learned that there is strength not only in diversity on a worldwide scale, but in cooperation and exchange.

As former International head Patterson recalls, the "first real test of solidarity and of the cohesiveness that was later to manifest itself in International" came when 3M Italy was being established in 1959.

Left without an inventory and without equipment with which to start business after a local distributor backed out of an agreement, Patterson, Harold B. Kosanke and others who were in Italy ready to start the company had to call on the 3M companies in the United Kingdom, Germany and France for help.

"At that time none of the people in our existing manufacturing companies in Europe knew the names of the people in the other two companies," Patterson recalled.

"Just overnight, literally, we were able to shake out a tape slitter from here and a churn (for making tape adhesive) from there. The other companies sent down their experts and we worked day and night in hotel lobbies in Milan. We had no office, no place to go. We worked where we could find a little cubbyhole. These fellows saw what the job was and they made up their own lists of what we needed in Italy and went back to their companies to dispatch the stuff to us.

"One fellow said, 'I'll make up a price list for coated abrasives' and another said, 'I'll do tape.' It was just

Children participate in an art contest using 3M tapes and other products at 1973 open house in 3M Germany's new head offices in Neuss. Below, managing director Dr. Wilhelm Nolden with bagpiper, albeit a German one, who gave the celebration a touch of "Scotch".

remarkable. The Germans, the French and the English all got to know each other and we made it.

"The result of those trials and tribulations was probably a good thing, in retrospect, because it taught everybody that we did have some muscle and if we all pull together, it could be done."

Later, as the International operations grew and spread from country to country throughout Europe and Latin America and into Africa and Asia, the interchange grew in many directions, in many ways.

Plants in the United Kingdom, France, Germany and Italy supply each other and all of the European Common Market countries with finished products.

The United States continues to be a major source of supply for all parts of the world, and the pattern and purpose of manufacture in other countries has been to serve the local market more efficiently and economically.

Yet, many export opportunities have developed for 3M's International companies. 3M France exports to 3M companies in Africa and Southeast Asia. 3M United Kingdom exports to New Zealand. 3M Canada exports to South Africa. 3M Brazil exports to other Latin American countries.

"All through the development of the operations we were trying to shuffle people from country to country and encourage global thinking within the company," Patterson said. "That, I suppose, was the cornerstone of our philosophy . . . It didn't make any difference who you

Tony Andres of the Philippines tries a new tape dispenser at a St. Paul conference. From left, Leo Allen, Jamaica; Spiro Voglis, Greece; and Herb Till, International.

Isaac Starkman, left, El Salvador, and Pedro Jimenez, Venezuela, exchange views in Minnesota with Lance Crowley of Building Service and Cleaning Products division.

"*Businessmen may not think of themselves as peacemongers, but that's what they are*"

were, it was how well you did your job, and we got everybody to believe that. We had Germans, Frenchmen, Japanese . . . everybody talking 3M philosophy."

Perhaps what Patterson was saying is not too unlike what Courtney Brown of Columbia University in New York said about multinational companies. ". . . Global companies, unlike political entities, operate in an environment in which their negotiations do not carry a heavy baggage of emotional commitment, but in which the resolutions are most often mutually beneficial to both parties in the transaction. These multinational corporations that have developed so quietly, but so suddenly, may be the hoped-for force that will ultimately provide a means of unifying and reconciling the aspirations of mankind."

Harry Heltzer, board chairman in the early 1970s, put it this way: "Businessmen may not always think of themselves as peacemongers. But that is what they are. And it's a title they can wear with pride."

Although 3M brought its own philosophies of business with it into each country where it established operations, it also knew it had to adapt to local conditions and live within the rules, regulations, traditions, customs and business patterns of the host country. It also knew it had to draw on the ideas and the expertise of the people it hired locally.

As Robert H. Stenberg, long-time International treasurer and an assistant treasurer of the parent company, said, "We have had some tremendous talent in the International companies and unless we gave them an opportunity to have responsibility and authority we wouldn't have been able to keep them."

People from the International companies stream steadily into world headquarters for training, to be updated on new products and programs and to give their input to the divisional people on what new products are needed in their markets and what new trends are developing.

Enthusiastic fans crowd behind a 3M sign at the 1972 Europe Cup soccer championship in Spain.

Not only products, people and information circulate in the company's cosmopolitan bloodstream. There's also a flow of the technology that has made 3M the diverse enterprise it is today. Research and development abilities are a critically vital resource for a high-technology enterprise and each fledgling International company immediately taps into the massive reservoir that originated in St. Paul and has been developed by 3M installations worldwide.

Each company, besides sending its key people to headquarters for training, has strong programs of on-the-job training and special courses to develop its people.

A top researcher in 3M Italy, Luigi Franchi, technical manager of Amateur Photo Products, noted that "3M offers a stimulating, demanding and rewarding climate in which to work." But he also pointed out that the opportunity for personal development through management seminars was an important reason why he liked working for 3M.

Besides the movement of people and the interdependence of activity, the solidarity and cohesiveness come through the support given to the International companies

by the International staff in St. Paul and Brussels, Belgium. The staff includes marketing and manufacturing experts in all product lines as well as specialists in finance, personnel, research and development, engineering, distribution and data processing. Their job is to ensure that their counterparts in the International companies receive the necessary information, training and guidance to carry out their task of making and marketing 3M products in their own countries and developing their own people. The International staff—considered "assigned" to the International Operations while reporting to top corporate management—is the liaison between International Operations and U.S. Operations.

When the International marketing organization was placed under the corporate product group vice-presidents in 1973, Leland B. Gehrke, International group vice president and later corporate vice president of finance, noted that "We have reached a point in our corporate development and in the growth of our international business where the early introduction of new products and greater penetration of markets outside the United States require direct and timely internal communications and a high degree of coordination among

Princess Christina of Sweden uses a 3M overhead projector in a talk for the Swedish Red Cross.

all supporting groups." In the past, the International staff marketing directors had reported directly to the International group vice president—now they became "assigned" to him.

In the organizational lineup of 1977, reporting directly to the president of International Operations were a corporate vice president for European Operations, which represents about two-thirds of the International business, and area vice presidents for each of three other areas—Africa, Australia-Asia-Canada, and Latin America. As 3M marked its 75th year, these positions were held by Manuel J. Monteiro, Richard S. Priebe, George L. Hegg and Livio D. DeSimone, respectively.

Most of the practices and policies that have worked successfully in building 3M's International Operations and made them thrive originated with the man who has been called the "father" of International, Clarence B. Sampair.

The 3M Board of Directors voted on February 13, 1951, to establish an International Division and develop 3M operations outside the United States. To Sampair, then 3M vice president in charge of production and industrial relations, fell the responsibility of forming 3M's International companies.

Sampair first became involved as a special advisor to Robert W. Young, the first president of International. A year later he became president of the division when Young was named chairman. Before 1951, Sampair had helped William L. McKnight staff the Durex organization, forerunner of 3M's own International operations, with 3M people.

Thwaits, Patterson and countless others who worked for and with Sampair credit this quiet and thoughtful man with the philosophies they found fit to follow, to embellish or to reinforce as the situation demanded.

"They couldn't have picked a better man than 'Sam' to do the job in other countries," said former chairman Heltzer. "Sam knew what the people we had in each country could do, what contributions they could make. You couldn't have gotten started without that concept.

"In the days when I was strictly product or group-oriented, it was easy to think that the managing director of an individual company wasn't giving the division or group a fair shake, and it took the education of overseas visits plus the counsel of Sampair and others to realize that managing directors have to be able to do a lot of different things in their countries and they don't have the staff available to them as we do here."

Sampair was known for inspiring people—not only the International staff people who were charged with helping establish and support the International companies but the local management as well.

"He had an uncanny ability to select individuals with leadership ability and to motivate people," said Robert Moline, who served as international manufacturing manager for tape, electrical and medical products in the 1950s and early 1960s.

Sampair, who served concurrently as executive vice president for the Tape and Gift Wrap division in the parent company for 10 years while he was head of International, himself expressed the view that a good manager should aim to please his customers and inspire his employees.

Some of the assets and people of two former Durex companies made up the nucleus of 3M's first International operations. They were acquired in 1951 after the court-ordered dissolution of Durex, which had been set up following 1920s enabling legislation by the U.S. Congress so that American industry could better compete overseas. The Durex Corporation was an American holding company owned by nine abrasives manufacturers, including 3M, that established manufacturing companies in England, Canada, Germany, Brazil and Australia. Durex Abrasives Corporation was set up by the same manufacturers in the same year, 1929, to export abrasives and other products under a common trademark to countries where Durex didn't manufacture. Sales companies were set up in France and Mexico by Durex Abrasives.

If Sampair was the "father" of 3M's International Operations, the pioneering McKnight was the "grandfather". The idea of developing a substantial international trade had always appealed to McKnight—who foresaw

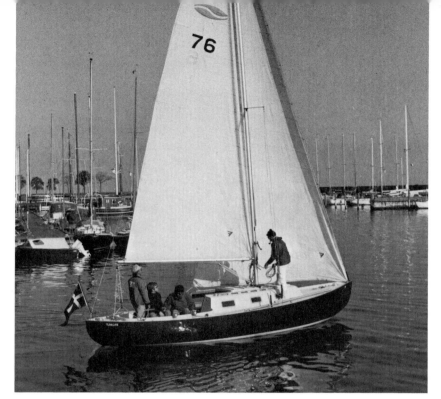

3M Club activities worldwide include sailing in Denmark.

International president Thwaits cuts a ribbon for June 1976 opening of newly purchased 3M Taiwan plant.

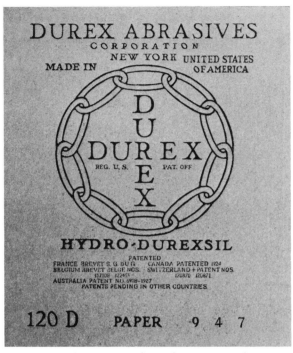

In Durex days, a number of U.S. manufacturers sold their sandpaper in international markets under a single brand.

that if 3M didn't develop these markets for its products its competitors would and would become stronger because of it. He also saw that there was a need that 3M could fulfill in other countries.

When 3M introduced "Wetordry" sandpaper, McKnight was convinced that 3M had a product that could compete with products from other countries and perform a unique function.

3M sent its eastern division sales manager, Robert H. Skillman, to Europe to establish distributorships for 3M products, particularly "Wetordry" sandpaper. From an inauspicious $189 start, sales leaped in a year to $69,391.

From the beginning, 3M had found that if a company were going to sell outside the United States, it had to have qualified people there. Often, it also had to manufacture there. In England, for example, the patents wouldn't be protected on products not manufactured there after a certain amount of time.

When the Durex companies were dissolved in 1951, 3M received the British, French, Brazilian and Mexican companies, as well as portions of the Canadian and German operations.

The dissolution of Durex had seemed a blow to 3M's hopes of international expansion. It was a blessing instead. New products were tumbling from 3M's laboratories and other Durex members were interested primarily in selling abrasives and tape.

At the same time, the Durex experience had given 3M a head start. "It would have taken the company much longer to get into international business if it didn't have the Durex nucleus at the beginning," said Calvin H. Corwin, who for some 36 years played a key role in launching and expanding manufacturing of 3M products in other countries. Corwin was a 3M engineer in St. Paul in the late 1920s when he was sent to England to set up what was to become the Durex plant there. After 11 years as director of Durex Abrasives, Ltd., in England and plant manager, he became vice president of production and engineering for the Durex Corporation. He served as vice president of production on 3M's International staff from 1951 until his retirement in 1964.

In addition to the experience gained through Durex,

In 1944, three "Millies" constituted 3M's international staff in St. Paul. From left, Jacobsen, Berg and Alvig.

Ray Herzog breaks ground in 1972 for new Sumitomo 3M office building. Shinto priest, right, took part in the ceremonies.

3M for two decades also had its own staff under the supervision of Mildred Jacobsen that handled various phases of export business and liaison with the Durex sales staff.

The breakup of Durex, says Sampair, "left us free to go our own way but it also created a big job to get properly represented in the important countries, both from a sales standpoint and from a manufacturing standpoint. We had the sandpaper plant in England, we got an empty building in Germany and a little plant in France which made tape by hand. In Brazil, the tape operation was bursting at the seams in a small building square in the center of Campinas with no extra land for expansion.

"For the first six or seven years in Europe, our big projects were the building of the French and the German companies," Sampair says. Two major acquisitions combined with 3M building programs firmly established those two companies within those first years.

The acquisitions—of an abrasives manufacturer in France which gave the company its first headquarters building and of an electrical products and paint manufacturer in Germany—also made it possible for those companies to borrow needed capital for new buildings.

"One of the things that 3M management in St. Paul insisted on was that we pay our own way in International Operations—and by borrowing on our own we did," Sampair said.

In Mexico, a manufacturing building was purchased. In Brazil, a new site was acquired and a new plant was built. In Canada, an old hangar and another building were leased while a new plant was constructed. 3M also wanted to retain the business it had built up under Durex in Australia where no assets had been acquired with the dissolution. Dick Priebe, an abrasives sales engineer, was sent to Australia in 1952 to start a 3M company there . . . out of his suitcase.

In establishing its own International operations, 3M management had made it clear from the beginning that it intended to build a global business.

43

"We feel we are building a solid foundation in our long-range plans to develop expanding markets for 3M around the world," 3M said in the 1952 annual report.

The formation of the International division in 1951 was considered so significant that the first press conference in the company's history was called to announce it.

Reaction from the investment community, which had only recently become aware of 3M's potential as a growth company, was mixed. One financial journal's wry question was: "Is 3M putting 'Scotch' on the rocks?"

The company, itself, didn't seem to be that sure. In mentioning the move in the 1950 annual report, the board chairman's letter to stockholders explained, "Rather than abandon profitable foreign markets for our products with the dissolution of The Durex Corporation, the directors felt this unusual situation justified our direct entry into world markets and our taking the risks involved."

It soon became apparent that 1951 had been an ideal time for 3M to set out on its own. World trade was beginning to expand rapidly.

The company had started fast and moved quickly in its race for many important global markets. From the $20 million in the International division's first full year of operation, sales climbed in five years to $66 million. That same year was the first in which profitable results were

3M microfilm systems speeded information retrieval when Norwegians voted in 1972 on Common Market referendum.

achieved in each of the eight countries where 3M had manufacturing subsidiaries. "Since our direct entry into world markets in 1951, the acceptance of 3M products throughout the world has exceeded our expectations," management told stockholders.

There was much more to come. International business in 1961 was seven times that of 1952. Twelve years later, international sales passed $1 billion. The question that had been posed by the financial journal in 1951 had been answered.

That kind of growth was accompanied by extraordinary expansion of both facilities and personnel.

Although the Durex people and facilities 3M acquired gave the company a head start, all of those plants, warehouses and offices combined were housed in only 600,000 square feet of space. Four years later, 3M had 14 factories in seven countries; and by 1960, 22 operations in 16 countries occupying more than 2½ million square feet.

This growth under the leadership of Sampair took place in various stages.

After the first seven companies were well on their way, what Sampair called "the second round" was started. 3M began to establish companies in the European countries where sales had been only on an export basis through distributors—Austria, Belgium, Denmark, Italy, the Netherlands, Norway, Sweden, Switzerland and Spain. As management had anticipated, sales multiplied at a much more rapid rate once 3M had its own organization on the scene. 3M Netherlands was established first in 1957 and by 1963 3M had subsidiaries in all those countries.

3M also had begun to expand in other parts of the world. 3M Argentina was formed in 1957; 3M South Africa in 1958; and operations were established in Japan in 1960. 3M Far East in Hong Kong became the first subsidiary in Southeast Asia in 1961.

Companies in many other countries soon followed.

Sampair drew freely upon 3M's resources to staff the international operations initially. Opening a new plant in another country inevitably meant bringing in a core of experienced U.S. personnel. Most of the Americans returned home once a start had been made. Nationals

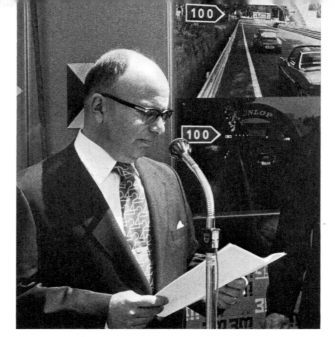

Managing director Peter Danos of 3M France tells the media how 3M reflective materials will aid drivers at 1973 LeMans auto race. Below, 3M "Oil Sorbent" material is used at refueling stations during 1974 LeMans.

3Mer John A. Kidd, second from left above, training distributor employees in Dakar, Senegal, to service a 3M copier in 1970. Right, John Marshall, China Affairs manager, stands on the Great Wall of China during mid-1970s trip.

assumed the bulk of the responsibility for operating the new company. In the mid-1970s, there were only about 100 Americans among the 34,000 employees in other countries.

"When entering the international market, many companies are content to send men of medium or second grade ability to carry out the operations; this was not true of Sampair," William L. McKnight said. "He selected top men in the parent company and sent them abroad to operate each international company. As a result, I think we have one of the most successful and well-managed international operations in the world."

Throughout the years of expansion under Sampair, he and other 3M executives frequently found themselves engaged in high-level business negotiations where they didn't know what the other side was saying except through an interpreter. Sampair's trips abroad—most of them by propeller plane—were many and frequent with very little time for sight-seeing. He recalls a few walks down the Champs Elysees in Paris, but that's about all.

Since the early 1960s most of the new companies have been established in developing, rather than industrialized, countries. In 1969, 3M even ventured into the Eastern European market, with a sales force operating out of a wholly owned subsidiary in Zug, Switzerland, and traveling into the Eastern countries. Like other U.S. based companies, 3M began selling to the People's Republic of China in 1972. A vice president for foreign venture projects, Lee M. Berlin, was charged in the 1970s with exploring opportunities for business in such areas.

In the 1950s and in the 1960s there were times when a single person, with a modest check from 3M headquarters in St. Paul "and a feeling about what will sell," as one 3Mer put it, went to a country to set up a company. He contacted the proper government agencies, set up a bank account, rented an office . . . placed a help wanted ad in the papers.

By the 1970s, 3M's international management was thoroughly evaluating the prospects of every country or region. It sent in a team of experts—engineering, manufacturing, legal and marketing people—to evaluate

Employees in Higashine, Japan, wear 3M-imprinted kimonos for a local festival performance.

Primed for new challenges and new beginnings in a changing world

a market. They studied the labor situation; the availability of raw materials, land and buildings; the political stability; the attitude of the government toward foreign investment; the means of transportation.

All of those factors became more crucial as 3M began establishing operations in countries that were not major economic powers or that did not have the same mix of industrial and commercial activity as those countries where 3M had experience.

As 3M's European vice president Monteiro said, "The world is much more sophisticated today and international business is much more complex. We need a team of people who can evaluate a market both in terms of their specialties and as businessmen who take an overview of the needs of people and 3M's ability to meet those needs."

Along with the continuing establishment of companies in the developing countries, 3M's International Operations also are entering a new phase in the well-established companies.

"We have now built viable bases in most countries of the world where it is practical for us to do business," 3M's International president Thwaits said on the occasion of the 25th anniversary of those operations. "We have a good solid subsidiary infrastructure; we have experienced 3M people; we've got great skills. Our challenge now is to get our market penetration up because, by and large, it is not equivalent to our market penetration in the United States."

In the company's 75th anniversary year he threw out another challenge to 3M's International companies—old and new—to create new businesses beyond those products, services and programs available from the United States.

"The continually expanding U.S. business base undoubtedly will be the major resource for our international growth for many years to come," Thwaits said. "Nevertheless, the size and sophistication of our Interna-

Brigitte Piotrowski measures expansion properties of electrical-products materials in Hamburg, West Germany laboratory.

3M Australia's headquarters building in Pymble, near Sydney.

tional operations and their diversified capabilities and resources, have prompted us to seek an added dimension to our pattern for growth."

Although St. Paul continues to be the source of most new 3M technologies and products outside of the photographic field, there are many products that in their final form were the design of a researcher in one of 3M's International companies.

For example, important developments in dry photocopying by 3M Germany are responsible for some of the copying machine production at the company's manufacturing plant in Cynthiana, Kentucky, U.S.A.

3M Italy scientists, expanding upon basic technology developed by 3M U.S. personnel, came up with a series of new electrical power cable terminations designed for areas where the air is heavily contaminated with salt from the sea or man-made pollutants. Applications for these terminations now are being found around the world, including U.S. coastal areas.

There seems to be no doubt that as 3M's International Operations embarks on the next quarter century, the roster of pioneers and innovators in the company is going to include names from more and more countries around the world. □

The mining company that didn't

American industry was booming. Manufacturers demanded abrasives. But Minnesota "corundum" wasn't the answer

It all started as a mistake in 1902, just one year after death had ended Queen Victoria's 64-year reign in England and one year before the first transcontinental automobile trip was accomplished in the United States, in two months, 10 days.

Early-day accounts say that a stage had just replaced the dogs and sled of mail carrier John Beargrease along the north shore of Lake Superior in the center of North America. An exciting discovery was made near the lake shore community of Two Harbors, Minnesota. Corundum. Next to diamonds, the hardest pure mineral in the world. Varieties of it went by the better known names of ruby, sapphire, emerald.

It seemed just the thing to sell to eastern manufacturers of grinding wheels. It *would have been* just the thing if the mineral really had been corundum.

Five enterprising Two Harbors businessmen—two railroaders, a physician, a meat-market operator and an attorney—joined forces to exploit the discovery. Each invested $1,000 and a new company was born in the summer of 1902, Minnesota Mining and Manufacturing. Ironic. The word manufacturing was included in the company name for reasons never explained. And, soon, the word mining, except for one brief venture years later, became meaningless.

The five men moved quickly to provide the "new abrasive" to eastern manufacturers. But they were not the first. They were beaten by 15 months by the Minnesota Abrasive Company, another group in the area enchanted by similar findings of what was believed to be corundum. However, to quote one report, the Minnesota Abrasive Company "soon became financially embarrassed." Minnesota Mining and Manufacturing took it over. Its own financial embarrassment was yet to come.

The founders first set summer 1903 for the start of production, then moved it back to fall. Yet enthusiasm held high. The Two Harbors newspaper reported: "The material (corundum) is there and its worth has been proven. The market is adequate for all that can be produced . . ."

It wasn't until the winter of 1903-4 that a quarrying plant was completed and the first trial extraction and processing of mineral accomplished, one ton, ready for sale. But how to get it from the mine site—named Crystal Bay by the five men, a name it has to this day—to Two Harbors with Lake Superior closed to shipping by winter? Teamsters said they would cart the mineral out and then never showed up. One man asked $20 a ton to get it to Two Harbors, just about the market price for the product. Finally, two of the founders hitched up a team and brought it down themselves.

The new company was in business. The plant at Crystal Bay was working at capacity. A sales agent was hired in Chicago and a warehouse leased. The first sale, a ton, was made in March 1904.

It was also the last sale. Two and a half tons more were ready to be sold. The founding directors held their second annual meeting and, with no money in the bank, voted themselves fine salaries: $3,000 for the president, $3,600 for the general manager; $2,400 for the secretary and counsel; $2,100 for the treasurer; $1,200 for the assistant general manager.

But, to quote one observer, "reality soon closed in." Several months passed and no more sales were made. Four of the handsome salaries were abolished. The general manager's was reduced to half. The Chicago sales office was moved to cheaper quarters—and then closed.

The board met. Employees in Crystal Bay were owed $347.25 in back salaries. A Duluth lumber firm wanted the $987.25 due it. Allis-Chalmers, which had provided much of the machinery for the quarry, demanded payment of a $1,038 promissory note. The minutes of the meeting noted, "No definite conclusions (have) been reached . . ."

The firm kept stumbling along. Salaries were paid by the directors personally. Allis-Chalmers was persuaded to extend its note. The board offered to sell some of its own stock at a loss to raise funds. There were no buyers. By late 1904, on the barroom "exchange," 3M stock had fallen to two shares for one shot of cheap whiskey.

Secretary John Dwan wrote to a friend, Edgar B. Ober of St. Paul, a railroad freight agent who had been one of the more optimistic investors in 3M's very first stock offering with $5,000.

Original 3M plant on the north shore of Lake Superior at Crystal Bay, Minnesota

Ober changed the course of 3M. The future, he judged, lay in manufacturing sandpaper.

Hermon W. Cable

John Dwan

William A. McGonagle

Henry S. Bryan + Dr. Budd at St Augustine

Henry S. Bryan, right, and Dr. J. Danley Budd, 3M's first president and vice president respectively, during a Florida vacation.

Would Ober, Dwan asked early in 1905, furnish working capital until the company could be put on a paying basis? The original stockholders had agreed to sell 60 percent of 3M's stock to anyone who would pay the company's debts and keep it in business. Ober believed that a need existed for a company to make sandpaper and abrasive wheels for the industry that was growing rapidly in the 45 United States. About $14,000 was required in immediate cash to settle debts. Twenty-five thousand dollars more, Ober judged, should be enough to start a sandpaper factory.

He didn't have the money. But a friend did, Lucius P. Ordway, vice president of Crane and Ordway, a St. Paul plumbing supply house. Ober went to see him immediately. Ordway agreed, the proposition was accepted and the two St. Paul men acquired control of 3M at the third annual meeting of the company in May 1905. Three of the original founders retired from the board. Two, Henry Bryan and William A. McGonagle, sold their full interest. A third, Dr. J. Danley Budd, retained part of his stock. Ober was elected president; he was to run the company because Ordway was busy with other activities. Ordway became first vice president. Dwan, the lawyer among the five founders, remained as secretary. Hermon Cable, the Two Harbors meat-market operator who had worked so hard as general manager during those first three years to start the mining venture and then to make it profitable, became second vice president.

Company letterhead in 1908 told about everything one had to know about 3M at that time.

Harriet Swailes, the company's first woman employee.

3M's first address: one room, second floor front, in Two Harbors.

Sandpaper sales rose. Expenses climbed faster. And stock offers failed.

Unsuccessful in their effort to mine and sell abrasive to eastern sandpaper manufacturers, founders decided to make sandpaper themselves. Old flour mill was leased in Duluth, right, until company moved to St. Paul in 1910. Below, C. C. Alliss, at an abrasive cutting machine.

Ordway invested the money Ober had asked. But Ordway had no idea how much more would be required before 3M became a functioning enterprise. And the illusion of valuable corundum was still to plague them.

The firm moved south to Duluth and converted an old flour mill into a sandpaper factory. A sandpaper-making expert was hired. He, too, optimistic about the worth of corundum and the sandpaper market in general, promised production during the final quarter of 1905 and profitability soon after. He was wrong. Costs mounted. Ordway's investment grew to $100,000.

Orders finally began to come in during January 1906. The first, $2. Then the Fort Madison Chair Company, $4. Income reached $291 the first month and by May was averaging $2,500 a month. Unfortunately, expenses were $9,000 a month. Ordway continued to lend the company money, but soon demanded that another form of backing be found. None could. The directors met in St. Paul in August to hear Ordway offer to sell his stock at a loss if necessary. Yet, as the fruitless search by other directors, chiefly Dwan and Cable, continued to seek new sources of financing, Ordway put more of his own funds in. His investment reached, then exceeded, $200,000.

"The business of the company is rapidly increasing," president Ober reported at a special stockholders meeting in Duluth November 24, 1906, ". . . and the only thing needed is additional money to carry on the business properly and to preserve . . . the company's credit." Still, no buyers for 3M stock could be found.

The manufacturing strategy of the struggling young firm was not working. 3M's competitors had important advantages: They were using domestic garnet as their abrasive—it was superior to imported garnet—and they controlled the supply; they were established with the major customers; all but one of them were closer to their markets. The 3M plan was to break into the market by selling the sandpaper that customers were used to— garnet and emery paper—to establish confidence in 3M's products and then to convert customers to corundum. Even the plant manager, a veteran of more than 20 years in making and selling abrasives, didn't know 3M's cache of "corundum" was worthless as a commercial abrasive. 3M was still stumbling down the wrong path laid out back in 1901 when the five optimistic businessmen saw a "new" future in the abrasives industry waiting for them in the ground at Crystal Bay.

The company manufactured huge quantities of "corundum" sandpaper before anyone realized the mineral was of inferior quality. But instead of stopping, 3M explored the possibility of mining a better grade of mineral from northern Minnesota to mix with the Crystal Bay rock. That idea, too, failed.

Finally, everyone realized the Crystal Bay mineral was worthless as an abrasive. Remarkably, no one considered giving up. Ordway became president and Ober vice president, both without pay in an attempt to keep expenses as low as possible. The next two years, retrospectively, were to become most important for the hiring of two employees who were to have great influence on

Edgar B. Ober, 3M president for 21 years, received no compensation during first 11 of them. Below, prospective investors visit Crystal Bay mining site.

A rough life

"I once had a barber who asked what I did for a living," recalls John M. Pitblado, since 1975 group vice president responsible for 3M's abrasives businesses.

"I told him I sold sandpaper and he started to laugh. When I asked what was wrong he said this was the second funniest occupation he had ever heard of. He also knew a fellow who raised worms.

"People could never understand how anyone could make a living selling sandpaper. But almost everything depends on a coated abrasive during some phase of its manufacture. Your eyeglasses, wrist watches, the printed circuit that's in a TV set, knitting needles . . . all require sandpaper."

Four of the seven divisions reporting to Pitblado on 3M's 75th anniversary day offered abrasive products to world markets, and each of the four is a more substantial operation than all of 3M was at any time in its first quarter-century.

Substantial investments by Lucius P. Ordway, St. Paul plumbing supply executive, carried 3M during its early years.
He served as the company's president from 1906 to 1909.

3M's future. Both refugees from their families' farms, they were William L. McKnight and Archibald Granville (soon and forever after known as A. G.) Bush.

McKnight, at loose ends after graduation from high school, knew only that he didn't want to follow his parents and his father's seven brothers into farming. He moved in with a sister in Duluth and attended a local business college, Duluth Business University. His course of study: penmanship, business letter writing and bookkeeping.

Five months through the six-month curriculum, McKnight was sent over to the new sandpaper company to be interviewed as an assistant bookkeeper. It was his second try at a job there. A year earlier, he had applied in vain for a laborer's job. But this time he was hired and began May 13, 1907 for $11.55 per week.

Bush had originally wanted to farm, but was driven off his parents' spread by his hay fever. He moved to Duluth to seek a pollen-free environment. He finished the program at Duluth Business University in a rush, four months—he attended day and night—and in August 1909 was hired to succeed McKnight as assistant bookkeeper at 3M. McKnight had been promoted to cost accountant.

The company continued to flounder. Ordway, busy, left matters to Ober. And Ober, still working as a railroad freight agent, delegated as many decisions as he could to the plant manager. The manager believed in cutting prices on sandpaper against Ordway's orders. 3M gained a reputation as price cutter that took years to end. The Chicago sales agent was unreliable. A poorly paid sales force resulted in high turnover. And, if some salesmen left with a bit of expense money unreturned—one kept $22—that, too, became a problem.

Ordway and Ober finally fired their plant manager and the Chicago sales agent. Cable became general manager, McKnight was moved to Chicago as office manager and another sales manager was named for Chicago. 3M had its foot in the door in the growing abrasive industry—sales were $192,000 in 1909—but the product remained poor and revenues went to keep the company operating and to begin to repay Ordway. Ordway and Ober changed jobs; Ober became president, a post he held until 1929.

Ordway also decided to move 3M from Duluth to St.

When Ordway insisted 3M be moved to St. Paul,
this building at Forest and Fauquier (now Bush Avenue)
became the first plant. It is still in use, Bldg. 1.

Paul. The high humidity in Duluth hampered the drying process of sandpaper—controlled drying ovens were years away—and Ordway also wanted to be able to watch operations more closely. Although 3M by then owed him close to a quarter of a million dollars, he paid the $35,302 cost of the construction of a three-story plant on Forest Street near Fauquier Street in St. Paul. "Ordway had to wait six months for the first payment of $300 on the building," a writer noted, "15 months for the next payment of $150 and another six months for the company to start reducing the debt regularly by $100 a month."

The plant opened in spring 1910 on a very discouraging note. A floor collapsed. A day before production was to begin, Bush and the new plant manager, Orson Hull, decided to take inventory of the 100-pound bags of abrasives shipped from Duluth. They had the bags stacked eight deep in the middle of the first floor, took the first inventory 3M had ever had and went home for the evening.

A new night watchman was on duty. If anything went wrong, he had orders to turn a crank which sounded an alarm in the American Delivery and Telegram office so help would be called. Shortly after midnight, the first floor gave way under the weight of the bags. The noise must have been frightening; not only did the watchman not stop on his way out to turn the crank or notify anyone, he disappeared for a week.

No one knew what to do about the inferior product. The making of sandpaper was neither an art nor a science in those days. Essentially, it seemed a simple matter: Take

McKnight and Bush, inexperienced in sales, intuitively realized they had to go beyond purchasing agents and talk to workmen.

paper or cloth, spread on glue and deposit crushed abrasives. Dry it, cut it up, and sell it.

Not that easy. 3M—and its competitors—by then had developed much of their own machinery for making sandpaper, taking it away from handwork, but that only seemed to speed up the rush to imperfection. It didn't solve the problem. Why did sandpaper turn out superbly one day and become limp and mushy the next? Why would some sheets last through repeated jobs as they should and others have the abrasive literally fall off the backing when put into use?

Variations as incredibly high as 1,000 percent in the quality of the sandpaper bedeviled all manufacturers. Workmen's vision usually was all the "quality-control" testing provided; if sandpaper looked good, it *must be* good. Some workers snapped a sheet next to their ears. If the sheet was brittle and snapped, it was assumed to be all right. No snap, it was too mushy and soft.

Workers blamed the glue, the paper, the weather, the gods. No one could explain why good sandpaper and poor sandpaper could result even when the raw ingredients all came from the same source, even the same containers.

3M's sales manager quit in frustration. Ober, also with some frustration, had to replace him. He had been impressed by McKnight's abilities and seven-day-a-week concern with the company's problems. He believed loyalty should be rewarded and named the bookkeeper/office manager, a man without any sales background, as national sales manager. McKnight was 24.

Sales experience may have had McKnight do what his competitors were doing when they called on potential customers: visit the front office and leave a catalog with the purchasing agent. McKnight reasoned differently: Wouldn't the workmen who actually used the product be able to give better, first-hand knowledge of their needs than purchasing agents? McKnight went off to Rockford, Illinois, and the city's 29 furniture plants.

Using a horse and buggy rented at $3 a day—it was faster getting around than waiting for a trolley—McKnight soon learned that potential customers, too—both front-office help and workmen—felt a "drummer's"

A desk maker owed 3M $16.84. He was delinquent. Sales manager A. G. Bush, here in national sales office in Chicago, received a new rolltop in trade.

place was in the front office. But McKnight, a soft-spoken, gentle man—not quite the typical salesman of the day—soon began to gain hearings in the work areas.

He had gained access to the workmen. But he still had a largely inferior product. Now he found it out first-hand. Even so, reports back to St. Paul, based on personal experience, brought no more benefit than the complaints of earlier 3M salesmen parroting the annoyance heard secondhand from purchasing agents.

McKnight trained his salesmen to do what he had learned could be done, get into work areas, find what kind of abrasive materials were best suited for customer needs, demonstrate 3M products and report problems precisely to the factory with samples of poor-quality sandpaper. McKnight also called for greater coordination between salesmen and the factory. He wrote persistently to Ober, pointing out problems as they occurred, and, finally, arguing that quality and uniformity, sadly lacking in 3M products, would be achieved only if a general manager were named to supervise both production and sales and bring them closer together.

Ober agreed—and selected McKnight for the job. One of the first acts of the new general manager was to name Bush sales manager.

Bush believed in McKnight's sales policies, followed and expanded on them. McKnight, for example, had arranged for several well-regarded industrial distributors to sell 3M products with their other lines. Bush took that one step further. He wanted the distributors' salesmen to treat 3M's abrasives as more than just another item in their arsenal. He further wanted those salesmen to follow 3M's policy of demonstrating their products to the men who worked with them and, at the same time, collecting their comments about the products. He arranged for 3M salesmen to accompany the distributors' men. The teams worked on customer problems together.

The effort succeeded beyond even Bush's hopes. The distributors' salesmen learned much more about 3M

For McKnight, 1916 was a big year. His daughter, Virginia, was born. Ober's temporary departure from St. Paul for health reasons, left McKnight, at 29, in charge of 3M.

products and thus sold more 3M products. One distributor even stopped selling the other products in his line to concentrate on 3M's.

It was 1914. The company was slowly becoming profitable. Monthly sales had reached an average of $22,000. Attention to quality was succeeding in lessening customer complaints. Even the debt to Ordway slowly was being reduced.

Then business virtually stopped. Everyone, without exception, who had been buying garnet sandpaper began to return the product. The sole and gigantic complaint: The garnet abrasive dropped off the backing as soon as it began to be used in the shops.

No one had any idea what was wrong. Men in all departments, within the factory and in the field, sought answers and came up empty.

Weeks went by as rejects mounted. Ober, McKnight, Bush—all felt helpless. One evening, a workman noticed an oily film on water standing in a scrub pail. At the bottom of the pail: a small amount of crushed garnet that had been mopped up from the floor by a maintenance man.

The workman called plant superintendent Hull. He couldn't understand the presence of the oil. The unused garnet in inventory was checked and didn't show any evidence of oil contamination. But if the oil were coming from the crushed garnet in the pail of water, it might explain why the garnet was falling off the sandpaper. Glue would not stick to an oily surface. If the crushed garnet used as abrasive on the paper were contaminated with oil, it would pull out of the glue in the finished sandpaper after a few minutes' use, just as customers had reported.

Hull investigated. He crushed and graded garnet from inventory to sandpaper-grit size and dropped the bits into a glass of water. An oil film formed on the surface. The garnet was unfit for sandpaper.

How could oil have gotten into the stock of uncrushed garnet? Had it happened before 3M received the garnet, which came from Spain, or had it happened at the plant? Would each new supply of garnet be contaminated in the same way?

The answer was found quickly. Months earlier, a

Spanish steamer bound for America with a principal cargo of olive oil ran into a major storm at sea. As the vessel pitched, some of the casks of oil broke open. The oil leaked into nearby sacks of garnet enroute to 3M. No one realized any damage had been done. The incident went unreported. By the time the garnet reached St. Paul, it bore no outward evidence of contamination.

But 3M had 200 tons of oil-soaked garnet on hand. It could not afford to discard them. Damages could not be collected to offset their loss. The company had to find a way to make the abrasive usable.

After months of experimentation, while poor-quality sandpaper continued to be made and complaints continued to be received, Hull found that a combination of washing and then heating thin layers of crushed garnet rid it of the oil. The balance of the contaminated stock had to go through this time consuming process, but it could be used.

McKnight did not want the "olive oil" problem or any variant of it to recur. He ordered the company's first laboratory to be established in a small, closet-like room—if a visitor wanted to come in, the lab worker had to step outside—where tests would be performed on raw materials, coated abrasives at various stages of manufacture and on finished products. Of course, the tests were crude and the equipment unsophisticated by today's standards. When an icebox was purchased to be used in conjunction with a newly developed glue jel test, it was considered a major research investment. (It also doubled as refrigerated storage for employees' lunches.) Total cost for the lab: $500.

Laboratory tests on products were elementary: rub, mineral distribution, glue and tensile trials. The equipment: a scale, hydraulic tensile tester, several rubbing blocks, pipettes, a treadle-operated tin shears and numerous tin pails to hold hot water for the glue tests.

Problems slowed use of the laboratory. Production men, who learned their skills the hard way, "didn't need research experts" to tell them how to do their jobs. McKnight wanted them to make use of the new lab, but they couldn't be alienated. They were loyal and hard workers who would have been difficult to replace. Nine research men came and left during the first nine months of the lab's existence. Finally, in October 1916, a recent high school graduate named Bill Vievering was hired. He had no chemical or technical training, but he could get along with people beautifully. He became 3M's first technical employee.

Each run of sandpaper was coded and the code numbers to label the runs had to be made up from this combination of letters and numbers:

C O M P L A I N T S
1 2 3 4 5 6 7 8 9 0

A not-very-casual reminder to plant employees of what management thought of inferior sandpaper.

The moving assembly line—Henry Ford's contribution to increased productivity—was being imitated within months by a growing number of American industries. The need mounted for more durable coated abrasives. Up to then, abrasives had been used primarily in woodworking. Now they were needed to finish metal parts on assembly lines. Sanding materials that worked well on wood couldn't sand metal quickly enough to keep assembly lines moving.

For months, experiments had been under way at 3M on the development of a new abrasive cloth made with an artificial mineral, aluminum oxide. The company finally developed "Three-M-Ite" coated abrasives, a product that remains in the line today.

Although "Three-M-Ite" was not the first abrasive coated with an artificial mineral to reach the market, it quickly earned the reputation of being the best for metalworking.

After an initial order for 20 reams was placed by car-maker Briggs Manufacturing Company in Detroit, 3M began to bask in a new and, for it, novel sensation: success.

In two years, gross sales doubled. In the last quarter of 1916, the board of directors declared a dividend of six cents per share on almost 225,000 shares of common stock held by 193 shareowners. 3M has not missed a quarterly dividend payment since.

The mistake of Crystal Bay had been corrected—permanently. □

A happy ending for the Crystal Bay corundum mine site. Campers know it today as Baptism River State Park, which includes acreage donated by 3M in 1947.

From adversity to diversity

The curiosity of an absent-minded ink maker and
the persistence of a banjo-strumming technician play a part

"Three-M-Ite" abrasives were a symbolic new beginning for 3M. The development and success of that product seemed to signal an extraordinary reversal in the fortunes of a company that had struggled to survive its first dozen years.

Until then, 3M had just three saleable abrasive products: flint papers, emery cloth and garnet abrasives. In the second decade of the young company's life, two more significant coated abrasive introductions were made, "Three-M-Ite" and "Wetordry" abrasives.

Then two new products popped forth unexpectedly and almost in tandem in the final half of the 1920s: "Scotch" brand masking and cellophane tapes. Together, they helped insure that the dream for 3M of a small and resolute handful of Midwestern industrial workers would become a reality.

The post-World War I League of Nations was holding its first meeting in Geneva, Switzerland, in January 1920 when a letter from a small Philadelphia manufacturer of printing inks, Francis G. Okie, arrived in St. Paul. He asked for samples of every mineral grit size used by 3M in making its abrasives. That letter, coupled with 3M's new but limited funds for research, was to have a profound effect on the future of the company.

3M wasn't in the business of supplying bulk minerals and the letter could have ended in a wastebasket. But vice president McKnight, who received the letter, was curious. Why had Okie written to 3M and not to a mineral supply house?

As a result of McKnight's curiosity, 3M was able to develop a new abrasive for wet sanding.

It was the first coated abrasive of its kind. And it soon propelled 3M into a position of world stature in the industry, while also improving worker health conditions and helping the auto industry solve serious production problems.

McKnight's handling of Okie's request changed the course of 3M's history. He instructed eastern division sales manager R. H. Skillman to learn why Okie wanted grit samples.

Skillman found an earnest young man in a small Philadelphia shop, working on an idea unrelated to the printing-ink business. But it was related to 3M's business. Okie had ideas for a new kind of waterproof sandpaper.

The sales manager recognized the potential of a waterproof sandpaper. Two major problems of smoothing painted or varnished surfaces might be eliminated—the problem of sandpaper loading or clogging, which greatly reduced the useful life of dry sandpaper, and the health hazards of dust in the workplace, a factor in the high labor turnover in dry-sanding departments of factories. Furthermore, there was a likelihood that smoother surfaces could be achieved by wet abrading.

Sitting with Okie in a clutter of test materials at an old, wood desk, Skillman expressed interest in Okie's ideas. With the inventor's permission, he wired McKnight to come to Philadelphia to talk to Okie about patent rights. McKnight came and he, too, met with Okie across the

Why does an ink maker want minerals? McKnight, right, asked R. H. Skillman to investigate. Result: 3M's waterproof sandpaper.

"Wetordry" waterproof sandpaper was warmly accepted by the auto industry. Workmen are hand sanding early 1920s models.

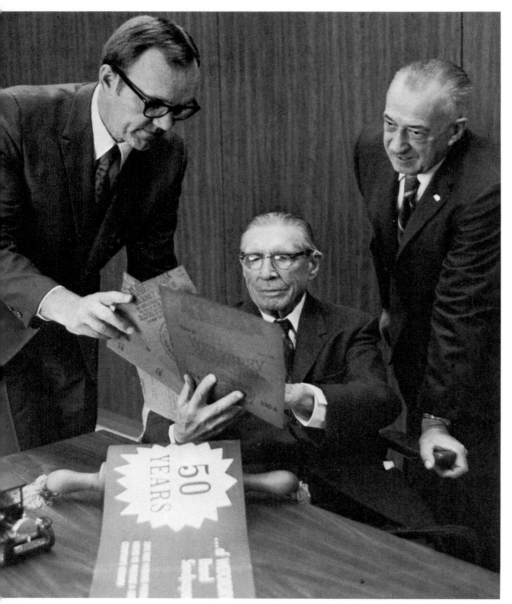

Francis G. Okie, center, 91, reminiscing about development of "Wetordry" sandpaper 50 years later in 1971 with S. W. Thiele, left, and Henry F. Buetow.

battered desk and was impressed with the man's ideas.

An agreement was drawn up between 3M and Okie February 3, 1921, which was to make 3M a leader in its earliest business. The company had found a "first," a new product which industry needed and would buy in quantity, one that could return enough profits to fund improvements, growth and development.

How did a printing-ink maker happen to search for a waterproof abrasive?

"We made printing ink on the second floor of an old building," Okie was to say later. "Our second-floor neighbor beveled glass for a living. He used a grinding wheel and there was considerable dust connected with the grinding. I often stopped in to visit with him, and one day he mentioned something about wanting to get out of the glass-beveling business. I wondered why.

"But as I watched him working, I noticed the dust he had to breathe and realized that this probably had something to do with his wanting to sell. After talking with him, I began to wonder why a person couldn't make a waterproof abrasive, a sandpaper that could be used with water. This would eliminate dust from abrading.

"I decided to experiment. I had to find out if there was such a thing as waterproof sandpaper on the market. I went to one of the oldest varnish makers in America— they were sandpaper jobbers as well—and asked to buy waterproof sandpaper. The clerk said there was no such thing.

"Then I went to work. I bought small packages of mineral. I mixed the adhesive, spread it by hand onto paper backing, and sprinkled garnet on it. I had my neighbor, the glass beveler, try it. I also tested it by sanding boards in my own shop.

"When I was convinced I had something, I went to a competitor of 3M's, and asked them to make a trial run of sandpaper for me using my bonding agent. They agreed. The sandpaper they turned out further convinced me I had a saleable product. Funny thing, they never asked me why I wanted the sandpaper or what I was doing with it.

"Then I got some people interested in backing me and when I couldn't get any mineral in the east, I wrote Minnesota Mining."

Serendipity? Perhaps. If so, it was the first of many such stories in 3M's heritage. It took place about the time 3M hired its first technical person with a college degree, Richard P. Carlton. Later a 3M president, Carlton was quick to admit that many 3M developments were the result of stumbling into things. But he was equally quick to add that you can stumble "only when you're moving."

3M immediately began production of waterproof sandpaper. which Ober suggested should be trademarked, "Wetordry."

McKnight, anxious to develop as much patent protection as possible for the risky new venture, contacted local attorneys. They could see little possibility for patents on the new product.

Undaunted, McKnight turned to Paul Carpenter, a Chicago patent attorney who had represented 3M on an earlier patent matter. Carpenter agreed to explore patent opportunities for the "Wetordry" product and was able to develop worldwide patent protection for it.

Carpenter continued to work with 3M on patent matters, full time in later years and much later his enlarged firm of patent attorneys was incorporated with 3M's legal affairs staff. McKnight spoke often of the importance of patents and trademarks, observing that "the patent consciousness and the success the company has had in the use of patents can be largely credited to Paul Carpenter."

At first Okie stayed in Philadelphia, mixing the waterproof binder there and shipping it to St. Paul in five-gallon buckets. Dozens of buckets of binder were needed for a single run of the new sandpaper. By May 1921, samples were sent to customers. The first sales were made in the same month to auto manufacturers eager to try out any product which might solve their painting and finishing problems.

The following year Okie moved to St. Paul. Life in the factory became considerably enlivened. 3M employees had never had an authentic inventor in their midst and although Okie was quiet and softspoken, he was different.

"Okie was a brilliant man, but he was terribly absent-minded," recalls purchasing agent Chet Powell, a 3Mer for 44 years. "There would often be eight to 10 hats hanging in his office because he forgot to wear them home. One day I gave him a ride home from the plant because he couldn't remember where he'd parked his car. This happened two or three times in the same week, and finally his family had to come and drive all three cars home."

Okie hated to be "confined to the specific," Powell notes, and many times this was revealed in his experiments.

He would mix experimental batches of waterproof adhesive in a huge washtub, for example, until someone thought to have him make smaller, more economical tests in a washbowl. When he mixed a sample of adhesive, he often failed to record the amount of each ingredient used. Consequently, when an experiment was a success, he didn't know exactly why, nor could he repeat it precisely.

Sandpaper goes retail, circa 1923.

"The wonder sandpaper of many uses": Auto paint shops and hardware stores soon began to sell "Wetordry" sheets to individuals.

A laboratory assistant was assigned to him to measure and record all ingredients used.

3M quickly realized the Okie formula had serious defects. Lab tests and field trials showed that the mineral rubbed off too soon and the paper backing disintegrated too quickly. Competitors were now experimenting with waterproof sandpaper. The remedy of these defects became urgent.

The solution: the paper backing also had to be waterproofed and a sizing coat of waterproof binder had to be added on top of the mineral.

The automobile industry found the new sandpaper to be what it needed and two major markets developed, car manufacturing and auto refinishing.

One of 3M's eastern salesmen, Joseph C. Duke, later a company director, made the first call on an auto paint shop. Duke found the auto painter using the traditional pumice to rub down the car. He wasn't receptive to a demonstration of waterproof sandpaper. ("The 'sand' will come off," the painter insisted.) He admitted pumice got into the crevices of the car and had to be scraped out and that the pumice sometimes cut deeper into the surface than he wanted it to.

But he finally agreed to a demonstration and when Duke finished sanding the surface, the painter's response was immediate. "Come here!" he yelled to his helper. "This man's got something."

The painter was so excited about "Wetordry" sandpaper that he placed an order on the spot and told Duke the product would sell to every car painter in Philadelphia.

"We grabbed a phone book," Duke said later, "found a whole slew of painters to call on and, as the man said, each placed an order. 3M soon was calling on shops all over the country."

At the same time, salesmen were persuading more automobile makers that 3M had the answer to their finishing problems. Waterproof sandpaper could be used with either water or oil, which cut down the friction heat and allowed workmen to produce a smoother finish on the new cars. It also cut faster under lubrication than dry sandpaper.

With newly developed lacquer and the novel sanding

Employees of the mid-20s convert jumbo rolls of coated abrasives into sheets of different sizes before packaging for industrial, retail use.

NAME	OCCUPATION	TIME	RATE	AMOUNT		$10.	$5.	$1.	50c	25c	10c	5c	1c
J.E.Cable	Cashier	310	175 /310	175	00	17	1						
H.E.Swailes	Steno	310	85/310	85	00	8	1						
Miss Ritt	do	60	50/310	9	68		1	4	1		1	1	3
Miss H. Dahm	do	240	60/310	46	45	4	1	1		1	2		
Marie Morressey	do	310	30/310	30	00	3							
Henry Blodgett	Stock clerk	310	60/310	60	00	6							
Paul Phillips	Bookkeeper	310	60/310	60	00	6							
Geol Heidemann	Clerk	310	50/310	50	00	5							
Wm. Vivering,Che	Chemist	310	40/310	40	00	4							
O. A. Hull	Supt	310	200/310	200	00	20							
Chas Alliss	Asst supt	310	140/310	140	00	14							
				896	13	87	4	5	1	1	3	1	3

MINNESOTA MINING & MFG. CO., Pay Roll for ~~MONTH~~ WEEK ending January 31, 1917 191

St. Paul's salaried payroll on January 31, 1917 exclusive of company officers: $896.13.
Right-hand columns note number of bills, coins needed from bank.

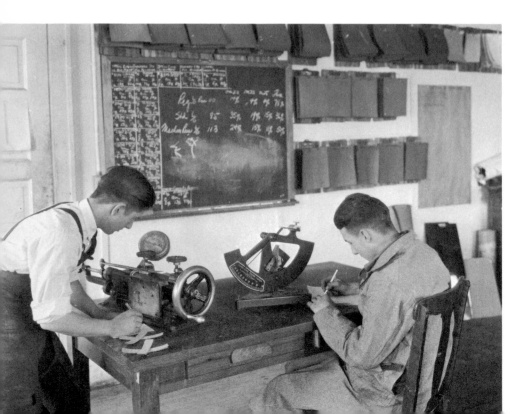

system, an auto body could be completed in three or four days, instead of requiring weeks of work as before.

Car manufacturers welcomed the new abrasive to their paint operations, where new primer undercoats and lacquer finishes were too hard to cut with the traditional rubbing bricks or pumice. "Wetordry" abrasives gave a smooth finish that polished to a high luster. Gradually, the new sandpaper replaced the old methods.

By 1926, manufacturers and auto paint shops were using the "Wetordry" product far more than any competing abrasives. Two competitors soon began to make waterproof sandpaper under license from 3M.

"Wetordry" sandpaper also improved working conditions for sanders in the body departments of auto plants. Before "Wetordry," attempts were made to control dust conditions with ventilators. Workers also wrapped cheesecloth around their heads to cover their noses and mouths. Both were unsatisfactory remedies for the

Abrasive laboratory technicians use best available equipment to assess quality of materials.

Market for the abrasive belts grew as 3Mers worked with machine developers. This early "swing grinder" is among many industrial advances on which coated abrasives methods engineers worked.

unsanitary and often dangerous dust conditions caused by dry sanding of car bodies.

Even with ventilators, workmen inhaled a certain amount of dust. As the automotive industry grew, lead poisoning contracted in body-sanding departments increased. Waterproof sandpaper eliminated the dust hazard.

Adapting the new product to the furniture industry took longer. The company realized that an abrasive with water as a lubricant was not satisfactory for use on furniture. But eventually 3M developed an abrasive sheet for furniture plants, employing oil as the chief lubricant for rubbing as well as a finishing system that would cut costs, improve the finish and speed production.

The new sanding system worked better at smoothing the new and harder varnish and lacquer finishes adopted by furniture makers and became widely used.

But the development of "Wetordry" abrasives did not change the fact that 3M remained through almost all of its first quarter century exclusively a manufacturer of coated abrasives.

When 3M did come up with its first successful non-abrasive product, it was a big one. Prohibition was still in effect in the flapper era when the forerunner of today's line of more than 600 pressure-sensitive adhesive tapes was born—rather improbably—in 1925.

This first successful move into product diversification came before there was an established new-product research program at 3M. There were no sophisticated laboratories dedicated to new knowledge. The company's lone "research" facility at that time concentrated heavily on running routine quality tests on incoming raw materials and outgoing abrasive products.

But the diversification was not an accident. It happened because 3M was alert to a customer's need.

The person largely responsible was Richard G. Drew, a

President Herbert P. Buetow, center, chairman McKnight, left, and inventor Drew with gold-core, two-billionth commercial-size roll of "Scotch" tape in 1957.

breezy, young laboratory technician who had worked his way through school by strumming a banjo in dance bands.

He dropped out of college in 1920 and began to work full-time in a dance band. Still interested in engineering, however, he enrolled in a correspondence course. He also watched the want ads. 3M at this time had decided to double the personnel of its research laboratory with an assistant to help on quality control.

Drew applied and was hired. He found his work at 3M far different from playing the banjo. He spent the first two years checking raw materials and running sandpaper tests. One of his jobs was to take samples of Okie's waterproof paper to auto shops around St. Paul for testing.

The two-tone paint finish on automobiles had just been introduced and was popular. Manufacturers were beginning to be sorry they had introduced the new style. Two-tone painting was causing headaches on production lines and even worse ones in small body-paint shops all

over the country. Drew solved the problems with his invention of what turned out to be "Scotch" brand masking tape, first of the now-famed family of "Scotch" products.

After being hired by William A. Vievering, 3M's first technical employee, Drew recalls working with Okie, making trial batches of waterproof sandpaper and taking the hand-made samples to a local auto paint shop for testing.

"One morning in 1923," Drew recalls, "I walked in and heard the choicest profanity I'd ever known."

Painters were cursing what happened when they masked a car for two-tone paint application with newspapers, butcher paper, improvised glues and surgical adhesive tape. The paint on a new Packard had just been damaged when paper was ripped off. With the brashness that came from being 23, Drew told the shop boss he would make something to solve the problem.

It took two years. It involved experimental efforts with vegetable oils, various resins, chicle, linseed, glue glycerin and different backings. One preliminary attempt was said to look like flypaper. There was a bleak time when some in management suggested that Drew drop the idea of solving the paint-masking problem and devote his full efforts to Okie and abrasives.

Returning to his original job, Drew remembered some treated, crepe paper left over from an earlier abrasives experiment. It provided a missing link in his search for a tape base that wouldn't allow the adhesive to get a firm grip on the back side.

The ability of the crepe backing to stretch and crepe—or wrinkle—kept it from full contact with other layers on the roll and solved the problem. The company's chief chemist was sent to Detroit with samples for car manufacturers. When he returned to 3M, he came directly to Drew. "You'd better learn how to make this stuff," he said. "I just sold three carloads."

The tape held tightly and stripped off well in the paint shops. Product modifications continued to overcome

Dick Drew, third from right, shown in 1925, with, from left: Percy Chamberlain, Ted Miller, John Sullivan, Tom Sayer, El Lund and Lloyd Hintz.

adhesive and backing problems, as reported from the field. But it finally worked. It was 1925, 3M's twenty-third year.

3M's masking tape was only five years old when Drew came up with another idea. This time he conceived the product that brought 3M not only new recognition in the business world but also global fame: "Scotch" cellophane tape, the filmy, sturdy, transparent tape for which the world discovered uses neither the inventor nor anyone else in 3M had in mind.

"Scotch" cellophane tape, like its predecessor, masking tape, came about because 3M was looking for the answer to the problems of its customers. Drew was trying to solve a packaging dilemma for a St. Paul firm which had an order for insulating several hundred railroad refrigerator cars. In trying to fill the order, the company learned that its batts of insulation would have to be wrapped and sealed to protect them against moisture in the refrigerator cars. It asked 3M to help.

Drew made repeated attempts to find a solution, all unsuccessful. Nothing was sufficiently watertight.

Meanwhile, Du Pont had come out with cellophane which made an immediate impact on the packaging market. The promise of the brittle, sparkling cellophane had been seen first by candy and cosmetic manufacturers and bakers. When Du Pont chemists made cellophane moistureproof, the product was adopted by meat packers, chewing gum manufacturers and other food distributors.

During Drew's experiments for the St. Paul insulating firm, another 3M researcher was considering packaging 3M's masking tape in cellophane to protect the rolls of tape from heat, cold, moisture and dryness. He showed Drew the cellophane.

Drew looked at it and thought, "Why couldn't that stuff be coated with adhesive and used as a sealing tape for the insulation slabs? It's moistureproof."

He ordered 100 yards of cellophane for experiments in June 1929. When it arrived, he cut the cellophane into

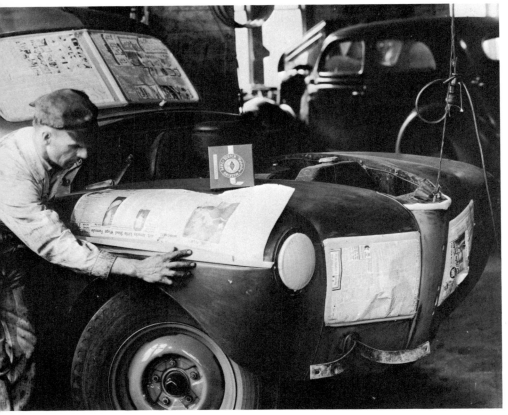

Product diversification: "Scotch" masking tape solved car painters' problems in mid-20s and remained in use as autos were streamlined.

great possibilities as an aid in packaging other products.

Research continued. It took more than a year before 3M had a saleable new tape, a comparatively short time for the development of such a successful product, but some of the longest and most discouraging months in 3M's history.

Cellophane didn't act like any other backing which 3M had used. It posed one problem after another. It curled near heat and split in the process of coating by machine. The adhesive wouldn't adhere evenly; bare spots were left in some places while other areas were too heavily coated.

At the end of each day, stacks of spoiled cellophane were piled several feet high on each side of the experimental coating machine. A truck was needed to cart away the daily waste.

Meanwhile, companies were approaching 3M for help in packaging their products. All wanted waterproof sealing tape. The companies using cellophane for packaging perishable food products were the most persistent of all.

No satisfactory means had been found for sealing these packages. String and rubber bands ruined eye appeal. Stapling was unattractive and awkward. *No* known way of sealing made a package moistureproof.

Slowly, 3M's production difficulties were overcome. It was found that if a primer coat was applied to the cellophane, the adhesive would hold evenly. Special machinery was designed to overcome splitting and breaking. New, virtually colorless adhesives were developed so coating wouldn't ruin the transparency of the cellophane.

Finally, on September 8, 1930, a roll of "Scotch" cellophane tape was sent to a prospective client. Two weeks later, the firm told 3M: "Your gum (adhesive) will adhere to glass or practically any surface. It needs no moistening or smearing and is so easily applied that it should be an ideal means of sealing moistureproof packages for cakes, cookies, etc.

"You should have no hesitancy in equipping yourself to put this product on the market economically. There will be a sufficient volume of sales to justify the expenditure."

six-inch widths so it could be pulled through the laboratory coating equipment.

Using masking tape's rubber-base adhesive, which was a dirty amber color, Drew coated several strips. Then he made the usual checks to determine if the adhesive-coated cellophane tape had possibilities.

The test showed cellophane could work as a backing for pressure-sensitive tape. Drew went on to try more samples in the hope of solving the difficulties of the insulation company. As it turned out, "Scotch" cellophane tape was not what they needed, but it showed

Even with encouragement from the trade, 3M was cautious. Only a brief statement appeared in the 1930 annual report: "During the year, a new product known as 'Scotch' Cellulose Tape was introduced. It consists of a cellophane coated with a transparent pressure-sensitive adhesive.

"Although it has many uses, its largest utility is in sealing packages wrapped in moistureproof cellophane. In view of the present popularity of cellophane as a wrapping medium, this market appears to have large possibilities."

The world was to show 3M just how large—despite the fact that a process for heat-sealing cellophane had been developed, thereby greatly reducing the demand for "Scotch" brand tape as a sealer for cellophane packages.

The new product entered the market during the first year of the Depression, a seemingly inopportune time for a "luxury" item. But Americans had been forced into thrift. They soon found the filmy, transparent tape could be used to make old things do. They discovered it could mend torn pages of books, window curtains, sheet music and even small rips in clothing.

"Scotch" origins

The company's most famous "Scotch" brand trademark is believed to have had its origin with an angry auto body painter in the mid-1920s, who, having trouble with the adhesion of an early roll of masking tape and noticing that the two-inch-wide roll had adhesive only on its edges, told a salesman, "Take this tape back to your stingy Scotch bosses and tell them to put more adhesive on it."

One person who left his University of Minnesota studies to join 3M in that era, is not sure it happened exactly that way.

"I seem to recall there was adhesive all over the back of the masking tape all right, not just along the edges," says Bert S. Cross, who later became president and chairman. "It was just a poor adhesive, and we improved it."

Whether the first batch of tape stuck or not, the name certainly did.

As the Depression deepened, new uses were found: fixing broken toys, sealing opened cans of evaporated or condensed milk, attaching labels to home-canned food. Insurance companies used it to repair torn policies, banks their torn currency, and all business found it convenient for mending torn documents.

Farmers found it handy for patching cracked turkey eggs, secretaries discovered it would patch torn fingernails, housewives found it helpful in removing lint from clothing, holding cheese on mousetraps and taping cracked plaster to the ceiling.

The major volume for the tape, however, was in the field for which it had been developed—packaging. Bakeries were the first large consumers. Then retail grocers learned vegetables, cookies and other foods kept better when wrapped in cellophane.

After relationships with bakeries and grocers were established, 3M surveyed the drug, dry goods, hardware, ready-to-wear, shoe and stationery stores to determine

"Scotch" brand tape line of products began to expand into home markets.

73

*A start toward tape
customer engineering: the
convenient dispenser*

*Customers like this one had problems with "Scotch"
cellophane tape until sales manager John Borden devised
a dispenser with a built-in cutter blade.*

additional outlets. 3M by then had developed a small roll for home use as well as its large commercial roll.

Salesmen discovered selling tape was just a matter of sending out enough men to cover "the territory." Almost everyone wanted the new tape.

Production and merchandising difficulties continued, however. The shelf life of the early tape was shortened by humidity, heat or cold. While the laboratory worked to overcome these difficulties, salesmen had to warn customers to keep the tape away from radiators and windows.

When the tape was introduced, there was no easy way to unwind it from the roll. The tape could not be kept free after a piece was cut or torn off; the loose end, rolled back in place on the roll, became almost invisible.

Small pieces often broke off and when a user succeeded in unwinding the necessary length, it had to be cut off with scissors—time consuming and awkward—or it had to be haphazardly torn crosswise.

The need for something better was essential. It took John Borden, "Scotch" cellophane tape sales manager, about 18 months of experimenting before he designed it—an efficient dispenser with a built-in cutter blade. The new dispenser allowed the tape to be unwound, cut off and applied in seconds. And it kept the end of the tape free for the next application.

It's estimated today that 90 percent of all U.S. homes use transparent tapes. Business and industry use tapes produced by six different 3M operating divisions. One variety, a special, gold, reflective version, is even "out of this world." It was used in a lunar landing vehicle as insulation against the temperature extremes of space.

Without realizing it, Drew had begun development of a product line which was to become indispensable—and, thanks to Borden, "dispensable"—in factories, homes and offices around the world. Most important to 3M, almost overnight it became an important source of earnings, seed money for ventures yet to come.

But it remained for Dick Drew to put everything in perspective. "Would there have been any masking or cellophane tape if it hadn't been for earlier 3M research on adhesive binders for 'Wetordry' abrasive paper? Probably not." □

Where we live

In large cities and small, 3M people share in the challenges and rewards of improving their communities

This company lives in a lot of different places — from Camarillo, U.S.A., to Caserta, Italy, from Sagamihara, Japan, to Saginaw, Michigan. In 40-some countries. On six continents. The men and women featured in the following pages work in one 3M plant, in Aberdeen, South Dakota, production center of a newer division, Occupational Health and Safety Products, formed in 3M's 75th year. But to the degree that any person can represent another, they are typical 3M employees, aware and proud of who they are and where they live and work. Like so many 3M men and women, they are also good citizens. On the job and off, they work in many ways to improve the quality of life for neighbors, for themselves and for distant customers.

Aberdeen plant employs a work force of close to 500. Right, where it receives its mail.

Rayme and John Schlichenmayer exchange "good morning" greetings.

RAYME
SCHLICHENMAYER

*A husband and wife, one a 3M employee,
spend their evenings teaching deaf children
and their parents to communicate*

Deaf children must learn sign language early — before that handicap leads to others. Their parents must be able to communicate with them. Rayme Schlichenmayer, who is partially deaf, and her husband, John, totally without hearing, open doors of life for Aberdeen children who, through birth defect or later injury, cannot hear. The couple also teach parents and college students who one day will work with the handicapped themselves. Both have full-time jobs, Rayme with 3M. John is also president of the Aberdeen Association for the Deaf. "We're making significant progress in convincing parents that the younger their children are when we begin to work with them, the more we can do," explains Rayme. "When they enter school, it's so late."

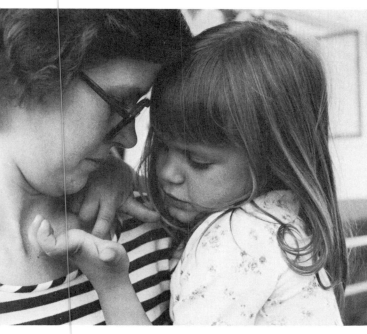

Kristin, four, Rayme and John's daughter,
has normal hearing, but has learned to "speak"
to her parents in sign language.

An assistant slitter operator, Rayme
also helps out elsewhere, as here
with label making.

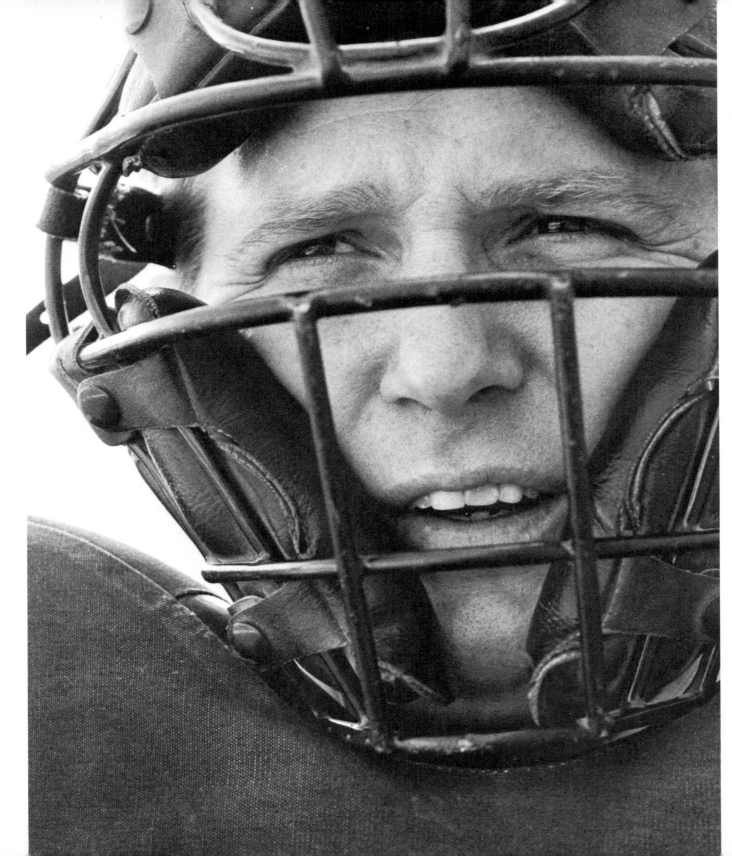

For umpire-manager Karst, right and facing page, bottom, baseball season is a hectic period. But he finds time to lead teenage and adult teams.

PAUL KARST

Summertime activity: Manager of two teams, president of a seven-club area league.

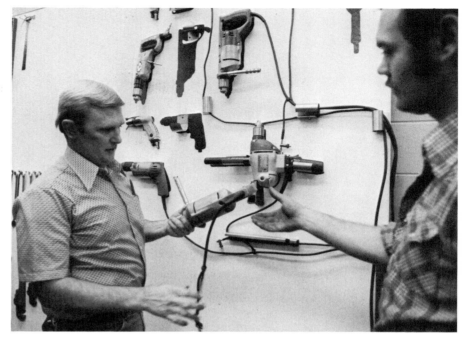

Baseball champions are made, not born. That's the counsel of stockroom analyst Paul Karst. He managed a teenage Groton team to a South Dakota title in 1976. Somehow he finds time during baseball season to serve as president of a city-county league that involves 180 boys from seven communities and also manage the Groton Independents, an adult team. His involvement becomes a family affair. Sons Daniel, seven, and Jason, five, are his bat boys. Kathryn, his wife, keeps them all company—and keeps the scorecard, as well.

Stockroom analyst Karst checks out tools to Richard LaBay.

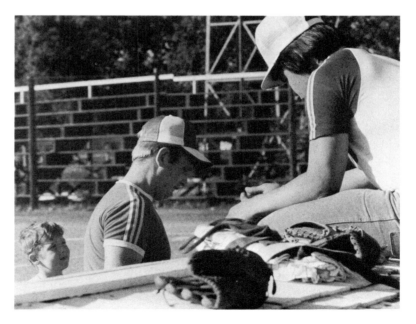

JIM, CRAIG, WAYNE AND OTHERS...

With United Way, youth groups and first-aid program

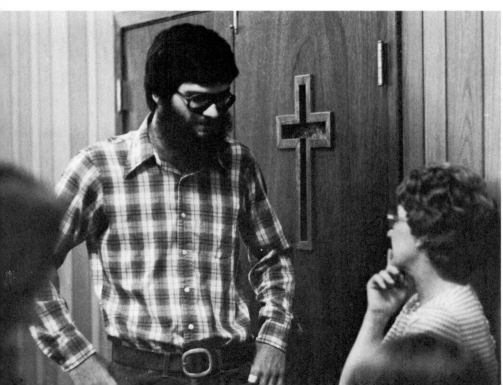

JIM JEVENS, second from left, plant personnel manager and United Way board member and treasurer, plots campaign strategy with 3Mers Al Hager, left, general supervisor, and Dale Crosier, second from right, process and industrial engineering supervisor, and Frank Bohall, executive director of the county United Way. Jevens also finds time for the city planning commission and St. Luke's Hospital Advisory Board.

CRAIG K. BOSTIAN may be the only lay minister who also is a preform cutter on 3M's graveyard shift. The job allows him to complete ordination studies while supporting his wife, Mary, and their two-year-old son, Jeremy. Craig works closely with local youth groups.

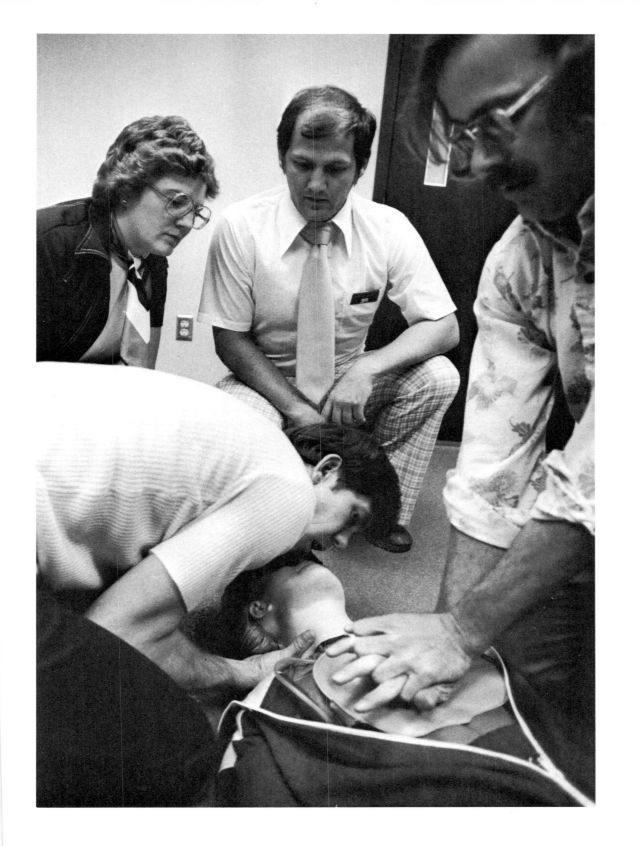

WAYNE KNOLL, center, personnel assistant and training coordinator, closely watches shift supervisors Curt Haaland, left, and Randy Hoff work on dummy in Cardiac-Pulmonary Resuscitation activity he directs for St. Luke's Hospital as part of a city-wide program. Shift supervisor Bonnie Fisher monitors. "First aid is a universal language," Knoll says. "It makes it possible for strangers to work together to save a life."

81

JOHN HUIE

More than safety masks are built in this community. Struggling young hospital benefits from 3Mer's efforts.

John Huie's grandfather helped to build the U.S. trans-continental railroad in the 1860s. Today, plant manager Huie helps build quality health care and education in Aberdeen. For the past two years, he has been a member of the Board of Governors of Dakota Midland Hospital, local, non-profit institution. He also is chairman of its finance, audit and purchasing committees and member of a joint conference committee with staff doctors. "We're a struggling hospital, trying to make it," he says. In addition to his hospital work, John is a member of the advisory board of Northern State College Business School, the YMCA board and a director of the Aberdeen Federal Savings and Loan Association. John joined 3M as a plant technician 20 years ago and moved up through process and industrial engineering while earning a college degree.

John Huie: plant manager and hospital builder

82

The Chamber of Commerce seeks Huie's views on special issues. Here, Huie with chamber's Larry Haugen.

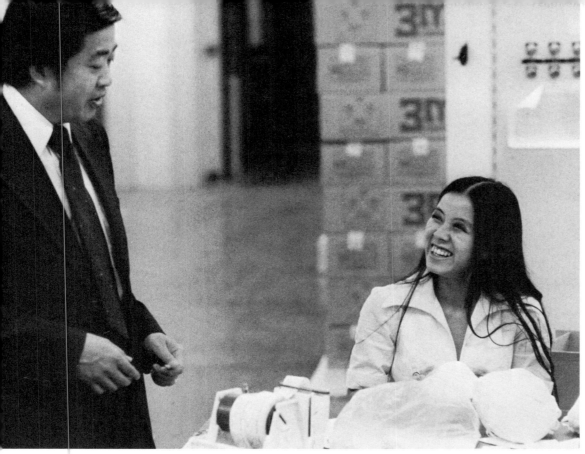

Lee Nguyen, one of two Laotian sisters at plant, inspects finished face masks.

Al Calhoun slits elastic material for face masks. Cordlike strands hold masks in place.

Slitter operator Mary Mattern lets her 3M Club membership show through.

Hospital administrator Philo Hall finds Huie goes beyond isolated board rooms. "When I begin to explain a situation to John," Hall says, "he stops me and asks, 'Please show me.'"

Making and marketing

*Festoons of
coated abrasives
in curing oven.*

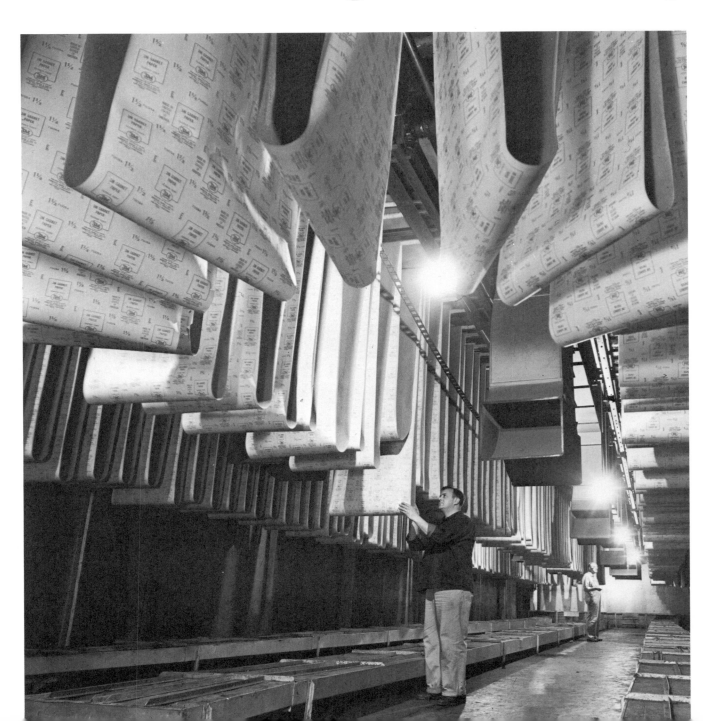

Creativity in the processes of production and in the customer-centered arena of sales and service

Among the many and varied M's of 3M Company — Minnesota, management, machines, microspheres, mistakes, and many meetings — manufacturing and marketing would have to rank high on the list.

Making and marketing, with research, are three major functions in each of the company's diverse businesses. A division vice president or general manager at 3M traditionally has three key lieutenants — a manufacturing director, a marketing director and a technical director.

As in research laboratories, the people in making and marketing do not work in isolation from the others in their division nor from their peers in other divisions. They share.

The sharing extends beyond the roles each function plays in the innovation necessary for a company's regeneration and growth. They also share improvements in the processes of production. They share plant space and capacity. They share markets and customers through the sale and promotion of related products. And they share information.

It has been said that the complexity of a corporation, as of the crystal, is three-dimensional. In similar manner, the operations of a 3M division have a tripod-like stability, based upon research, manufacturing and marketing.

There were fewer than two dozen salesmen covering the country for 3M when McKnight, as general manager, first urged a continuing exchange of information and ideas, interest and cooperation going both ways between the sales force and plant employees.

"Sales people must feel," he said, "that they are part of our factory and pass along ideas to the factory. The reverse also is true."

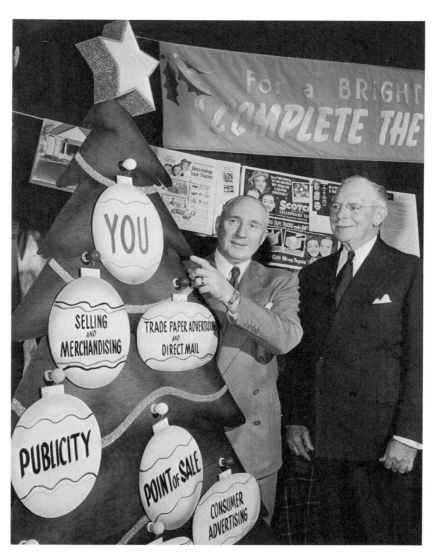

Early sales executives Louis F. Weyand and George H. Halpin tell assembled salespeople in 1952 about a most important element of customer service.

More recently other 3Mers have spoken of the false notion some may have that contact between research, production and marketing is made only briefly — at the points where the research runner passes the baton (a new product) to the manufacturer, who then gives it to a marketer who carries it on the final leg of a relay.

"If that's the only communications link between these functions, it's clearly not enough," L. W. Lehr said in a workshop for others interested in the health care market. "Our market researchers and our field sales personnel are constantly serving as extra eyes and ears for our research and production people."

Arizona operating room nurses in early 1977 heard it put another way when David J. Steveken of the Surgical Products division appeared with them as a workshop panelist: "The ability to listen is one quality we in business must have. And listening shouldn't end if we don't have the product you need; that's where it ought to begin."

That's how many things begin at 3M.

By listening to teachers and instructors around the world in the early 1970s, the makers and marketers of 3M's overhead transparency projectors learned that their ten-year-old product line could offer even more valuable communications tools if a way were found to cope with electrical codes and performance criteria that varied from market to market.

The variety of requirements had rendered the product line complex, more costly than necessary and difficult to make.

An intensive two-year effort, with close liaison between manufacturing, marketing and engineering, produced a new unit with total interchangeability of parts, and with price and performance characteristics that pleased the customers.

Price and performance help determine whether a new product or project will sink or swim in the marketplace.

In turn, the people in production determine, for the most part, whether the price will be right because manufacturing costs—raw material, wages and tools, plants and machines for the workers—usually are the largest component of a sales price.

With customer satisfaction and 3M success as their ultimate objective, the makers in 3M's world of work find adventure and challenge in four fields of continuing endeavor: prompt service to the buyer, quality assurance, control of manufacturing costs, and efficient use of resources, including the capital invested in plants and equipment.

The challenges and the excitement of meeting them become a personal matter for plant employees as they strive to reduce waste and do things right the first time. At the individual level, it can often be a matter of ounces, or seconds or inches — or less, where quality depends upon precision coating to the millionths of an inch. An ounce of extra effort in the making process can lead to satisfied customers in the marketplace. It can also result in dollars

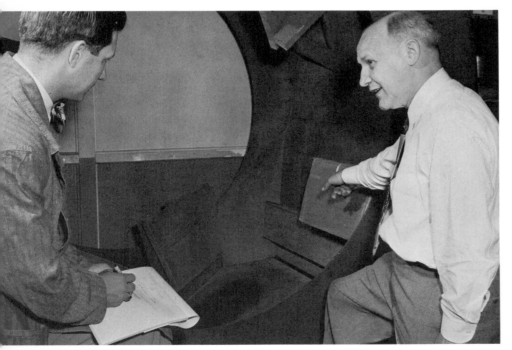

Helping to "build in" quality: William A. Vievering, right, first 3M laboratory employee in 1916, checks results in the late '40s of a tape packaging performance test made in a carton-tumbling "torture chamber."

saved for the improvement and expansion of production facilities, the wherewithal for creation of new jobs.

All in all, it's made for an exciting journey from that first, turn-of-the-century trial run of sandpaper near Lake Superior. In the first half of the 1970s, 3M was able to invest about $1 billion in new plants and equipment.

Along the way, many of the company's best-known

The many M's of 3M Company

The three M's of Minnesota Mining and Manufacturing Company have been used in various ways to refer to more than making and marketing. Abrasives and other products for auto-refinish trades were long promoted in advertising and direct mail by a fictional character named Mike M. Martin. The overall-clad model for the Mr. M.M.M. character was on hand once for a national meeting of the automotive trades sales force.

Early employee publications made a considerable to-do over marriages between two 3Mers, under the standing headline, "Ro-MMM-ances." Later, trade shows and professional exhibits often found health-care personnel dealing with hospital nuns and others who preferred non-alcoholic hospitality. This led to "Milk, Munch and Music" rooms where convention-weary delegates could relax as guests of 3M Company.

A group of 3Mers who vacationed annually at trout streams in Wyoming were surprised one year when their friendly, impish provisioner greeted them with a large, road-side sign in front of his general store: "We sell 3M products: Mustard, Margarine and Mayonnaise."

And on paydays—for employees, suppliers, tax collectors and shareholders—the three M's have been irreverently translated to stand for "Magic Money Machine."

Huge coating rollers, milled to extremely close tolerance in 3M machine shops, become part of the process for progress.

products made their pioneering production runs on the same equipment used to produce abrasives or other precision-coated products.

Early copy-machine papers were made on a machine which coated pressure-sensitive tapes. Duplicating-product coaters, in turn, were used to produce the first medical tapes. Reflective sheeting first came off a web-process maker designed and primarily used for other work.

When a new development is unrelated to other lines, it has frequently been necessary to begin with something less than optimum manufacturing conditions.

The manufacture of "Scotchlok" electrical connectors began in the corner of a tape plant at Hutchinson, Minnesota, where tape converting itself had begun in a war-surplus hemp warehouse. As business grew, the Hutchinson facilities grew to become a modern, multi-plant complex with clean-room conditions for the making of magnetic tape and a payroll for close to 2,000 employees.

Oldtimers recall the efforts in the 1930s to add a retail package of trim cement in tubes to an existing bulk adhesives business.

Employees took an ordinary kitchen pressure cooker, installed a petcock near the bottom, and drilled a hole through the top to insert an air supply hose. The cooker was filled with adhesive, the cover clamped and 10 pounds of pressure applied. When the lower valve was opened, adhesive flowed into the tubing.

Next problem: sealing the tube.

One of the workers on his way home noticed a grocer cutting plug tobacco with a small, hand guillotine. He bought one just like it and filed the blade to a blunt edge. With the dull guillotine, he was able to crimp shut the

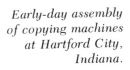

Early-day assembly of copying machines at Hartford City, Indiana.

ends of the tubing, and 3M had a shaky start in the retail adhesives business.

Successes of the '60s and '70s are less simple. Some call for a task force of technical talent from 3M's Manufacturing Council, an organization of division and staff manufacturing directors, most of them with prior experience on production lines or as plant managers. Their concerns range from process improvement to inventory control to resource conservation, including human resources—as shown in the task force priority given to the health, safety and development of workers.

Production scheduling is closely tied to marketing projections and both have an impact on inventory requirements for raw materials and finished goods.

In building, staffing and operating its plants, a 3M division can learn from other divisions and it can also call on a corporate staff of engineering and manufacturing specialists. They include the model-maker who builds a complex architectural miniature of a plant, sometimes with as many as 6,000 carefully coded parts for study and evaluation; the project engineer who will turn the approved model into a new plant, with complex mixing and milling and making equipment; the metrologist whose laboratory serves as 3M's internal bureau of standards, calibrating machines that gauge thicknesses down to .0000005 of an inch; the environmental engineer monitoring air and water quality before and after a new plant opens; and the expert in extrusion technology who takes apart an injection-molding machine to see if it can be made less expensively or modified to produce more efficiently.

"Our primary jobs," says Donald R. Guthrie, vice president, engineering and manufacturing, "are, first, to find building sites and then to build appropriate new plants, offices and laboratories; secondly, to constantly improve production processes so that the company can reduce manufacturing costs while it maintains or betters high product quality."

Some of the work is long range. Some is not, especially when the world is waiting for a newly announced product development.

A story is told about the long ago day when a 3M

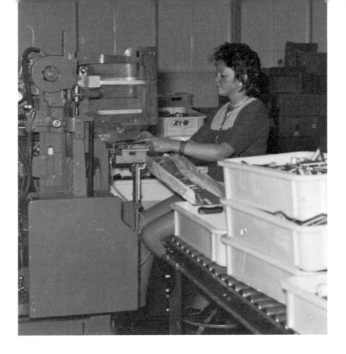

Cassette production in United Kingdom, left, and abrasives makers at work in France, below.

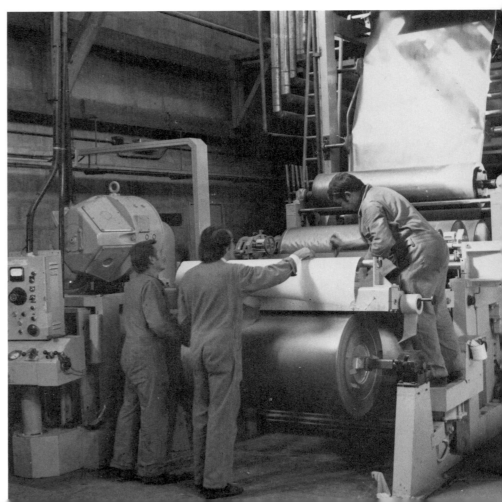

For the shelter market: Raw material for roofing granules at Belle Mead, New Jersey, in the early '60s.

researcher reported to management his successful fabrication, by hand, of a new and improved printing plate. A Saturday morning meeting was called for the following day and the inevitable question was asked. How much to build a pilot plant?

Guthrie estimated the cost.

Next question: How long would it take to build such a plant?

"Two months," Guthrie answered optimistically, believing the project to be a modest one and knowing full well that three to five years lead time was common for a major new plant.

The response was quick: "What are you trying to do, Don, make a career out of this one job?"

When a customer is waiting in the wings, the deadline pressures can be intense.

The decision to move from pilot plant to major new manufacturing facility involves substantial risk. And the risks involve more than money. Careers, community relations and customer satisfaction are also involved. Will a new process design live up to expectations? Will quality and unit cost requirements be met? Will inflation in material costs or wages lead to inefficiencies? Will the market still be there when the maker is ready?

A management team can evaluate these risks only through the close collaboration of manufacturing managers with their colleagues in marketing, research, finance and engineering.

Community relations were a consideration when 3M was seeking to expand its reflective sheeting output.

"I remember we were looking for a plant site and we recommended Guin, Alabama," says Cy Pesek, who was involved in much of 3M's physical growth from 1944 through 1969. "Everyone thought we had picked the wrong site."

Parts of rural America were just becoming industrialized and there was concern whether the hardworking men and women of the area, skilled in their own way through an agricultural heritage spanning generations, could adapt to factory work. The initial concern eased when the plant took shape and hiring began.

"Lyle Fisher, personnel officer at the time, told me," says Pesek, "that when the people of Guin came to the plant to inquire about employment, they interviewed us instead of the other way around. That seemed to us a pretty good sign. And, square foot for square foot, the plant we built there has been one of the most productive in all of 3M."

The territorial rights and responsibilities of 3M plant managers are not spelled out in great detail, yet they are respected by others in the company and in their communities. They can, as one author has observed, walk around a place and feel it is theirs, even though it does not actually belong to them, just as Buckingham Palace does not belong to the Queen nor the White House to the President.

They wear many hats and, with long service, can come to be recognized as "Mr. 3M" in their communities.

Lou Bohn, a plant manager for 25 years at Cumberland, Wisconsin, recalled in retirement how "you become active in the structure of the town and sometimes it seems that you're on the job seven days a week, 24 hours a day."

At the other end of the maker-to-market pipeline, 3M sales representatives have experienced similar rights and responsibilities in their assigned territories. And, as do the factory personnel, they employ the skills and talents of a supporting cast which includes specialists in market analysis, advertising and sales promotion, distribution and delivery systems, product publicity and technical service.

The "territory" of a 3M sales representative today can be anything from a few square miles in Manhattan to three or four states in the Great Plains or Rocky Mountain areas. It can be an entire country, with responsibility for all products, in new operations outside the United States.

One salesman whose career took him from the early days of train coach to jet travel was John F. Whitcomb.

"My first job as one of nine people in the New York sales office in 1934," he recalls, "was to answer the phone, take orders, write up the orders, take them out to the warehouse and help the warehouseman if it was a rush job, post all of the invoices, keep the stock records, order the stock from St. Paul, generally handle complaints and what-have-you. I can remember many nights working until 9 o'clock."

Whitcomb moved from the office to a sales territory in

Moving products to people: Warehouse supervisor Mary Doody, left, at the Chicago sales branch; below, a delivery van in Europe.

An early class, above, of electrical products sales representatives in the 1940s. Below: the voice of 3M in the person of Harriett Sinclair, St. Louis branch sales coordinator, processing orders as liaison between maker and market.

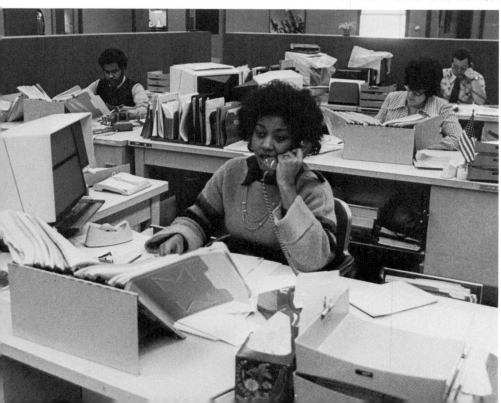

1938 and later became a vice president and director, but not before he reached an understanding on the role of sales people with Archie Bush, among the earliest of legendary 3M sales executives.

"I think it was 1943 when I made my first trip to a St. Paul sales meeting," Whitcomb says. "I was the youngest sales manager there and Bush in his pep talk said something to the effect that every sales manager should know where every one of his sales people is every moment of every day.

"You know, I could hardly stand it. Maybe I didn't understand him, but nobody can run a sales force that way. You have to have people who know how to run their own little businesses. You can only supervise them and give them a challenge, but you can't be with them all day.

"So I told Bush, in front of all those older sales managers; 'I don't agree with that at all.' Well, you've never seen Mr. Bush get so red. He looked at me and said: 'You're a pretty damn smart fellow. I'll tell you what I'm going to do. I'm going to come down to New York and teach you how to run a sales organization.' I figured that was the end of my job.

"But my boss, Al Butz, said, 'No, I think you're going to get along all right with Mr. Bush.' And, you know, I did, for the rest of his life."

Bush, Louis F. Weyand, Joseph C. Duke and George H. Halpin were among the earliest sales and marketing leaders at a time when 3M's only major market was "smokestack America."

Weyand recalls calling on the trade in the Midwest: "Plants started early, usually 7 or 7:30 a.m. and we did plenty of walking because they were scattered around the outskirts of towns. We had no cars, but sometimes we hired a horse and buggy at the local livery to haul our sandpaper samples."

Automobile, furniture and other factories were the target of most 3M sales and marketing efforts in the company's first 30 years.

D. W. Maher, a retired marketing vice president who started when every order had to be copied about a dozen times by Ditto machine and sent to the plant through pneumatic tubes, recalls how meticulous Weyand was about customer relations.

"He had a black book with countless birthdays, anniversaries and such," says Maher, "and each morning the first thing he would check his black book. When stationed in Detroit, he knew everybody in the General Motors building and a lot of people at Ford."

The first realization that 3M had potential beyond industrial markets came with the introduction of cellophane adhesive tape, and the discovery that this new product line did better when assigned to a separate sales force which wasn't concentrating on the big, established abrasives accounts.

Marketplace changes helped. When 3M was founded, many of the merchandise purchases by people in a predominantly rural America arrived by train or wagon, if they weren't picked up during a round-trip buggy ride to the county seat. Parcel post legislation in 1913, coinciding roughly with the beginnings of private car ownership, began the changes.

Manners and morals also changed in the World War I years and women emerged, after suffrage in 1920, as an increasingly influential group of buyers to be appealed to. Prosperity of the 1920s and tremendous growth in the circulation of national magazines created a direct market for some manufacturers that had never existed.

Large retail sales were not to exist for 3M until some time later, though sheets of sandpaper were offered early to the consuming public, and saxophone players of the Roaring Twenties may recall that 3M offered a retail pack of sandpaper strips for smoothing their reeds.

Still to come were the rise of specialized distribution channels, the supermarkets, the mass merchandising outlets and, within 3M, a wave of market-oriented product development and manufacturing expansion.

After 3M had entered new markets—electrical insulation and communications, office systems and equipment, imaging and graphic arts with materials for signing, printing and copying, education and government, health care —*Forbes* magazine was able to observe in the '60s:

"3M marketing operates on a simple principle that no market, no end product is so small as to be scorned; that with the proper organization, a myriad of small products can be as profitable, if not more so, than a few big ones. More firmly than most, 3M management appreciates that

the beach is composed of grains of sand, the ocean of drops of water."

The people involved continued to make their own luck.

Edward J. Kane, who became a 3M director and group vice president, recalls being hired as 3M's first printing products salesman at a time when there was only one product: a glass-bead coated paper called "Spherekote."

"Bert Cross was glad to find someone who at least knew what a printing press was," Kane says. "After working during the Depression as a longshoreman, I'd had some experience selling presses and printing inks. A little later we hired another sales person and Cross told me, 'Gee, you better be a supervisor,' and I became a sales supervisor with a sales force of one, Lee Norwich."

Two decades later, as a result of continuing collaboration between the makers, marketers and developers of printing products, 3M's progress was noted by the Public Printer of the United States, a user of 3M products on government printing presses. Speaking at the dedication of a new Printing Products division plant in Middleway, West Virginia, he suggested that from the time of Gutenberg to the time 3M entered the graphic arts field there had been less innovation than 3M alone had been responsible for in a few short years.

South Pole service call: Parka-clad Karl Marshall of 3M New Zealand visits the only continent without 3M operations to assist U.S. Navy personnel with routine copier maintenance.

Among those who had been listening and learning about customer needs was Allan J. Huber, hired to sell printing products in San Francisco in 1955 and later, managing director of 3M Germany. In 3M's 75th anniversary year, as the group vice president succeeding Ed Kane, he was back in Germany, heading 3M's substantial delegation to the largest graphics trade show ever held, DRUPA, an international exhibition held every five years, named by a contraction of the German words for "print" and "paper."

It has come as news to some outsiders over the years that 3M does not have a single corporate sales force, but instead many smaller sales forces with specific product knowledge and market responsibilities.

The way they have come to serve a number of markets throughout the country drew admiring comment from one business writer:

"Close the doors, they come in the windows. Close the windows, they come in the door. Whether they're pushing copying machines, perfumed tape, printing plates or soap pads, 3M's salesmen have a little something for everybody. No one single product is truly big in its own right. Added together they constitute a real growth company."

Through their alert presence in many markets, 3M sales representatives are often able to learn what customers will need, even before the customers know themselves.

Part of the "presence" consists of time and talent devoted to more than a thousand memberships in trade, technical, professional and business associations in the United States alone. This kind of closeness to markets has provided useful information about the needs of people and can result in better service . . . through better standards, more convenient trade shows and exhibits, more stimulating convention programs.

Participation has included leadership positions for many a 3Mer, in groups as varied as a Health Industry Association, Graphic Arts Technical Foundation, Business Equipment Manufacturers Association, National Office Products Association, American Supply & Machinery Manufacturers Association, and National Micrographics Association.

One typical result of such involvement: a "Man of the Year" citation from the International Tape Association for Dan E. Denham, a group vice president who years earlier had begun with 3M as a magnetic-tape salesman. During his career he served as president and board chairman of the group that honored him.

Recognition of a similar type went to dental products sales representative Deane W. Langguth when a state association of dental assistants granted him honorary membership for services contributing to their welfare. He was the fifth person so honored in the group's 56-year history.

In a firm as diversified as 3M is, service can take many forms.

Technical service which accompanies the sale of many 3M products can be as simple as a wall chart instructing auto-body shop workers on the use of a dust mask or instructions imprinted on a package of sandpaper for do-it-yourselfers.

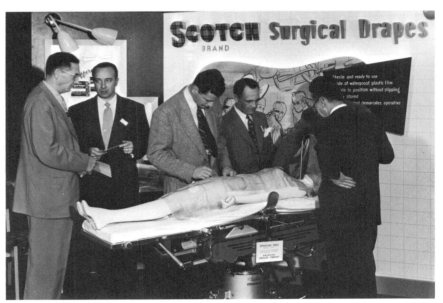

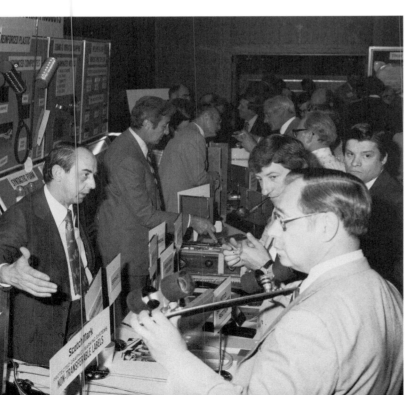

3M on display: Gene Ward, left, of Industrial Specialties division, gives a helping hand at product exhibit. Top left: magnetic recording tape at a convention in Germany. Top scene above: Design Engineering Show delegates crowd around 3Mer Cornelius S. Howard of the New Business Ventures division in 1974. Immediately above: L. W. Lehr, second from left, during 1950 Cleveland convention of the International College of Surgeons.

In some markets, the technical service is much more elaborate: Tape customer engineering specialists may actually design new equipment to solve a food processor's packaging problem; they develop about 50 new applications and custom solutions a month. Government workers overwhelmed with paperwork can visit special Microforum display rooms to find a 3M system that eases their burdens. Factory customers can bring samples to a coated abrasives methods center for help on special dimensioning, machining and finishing problems. And health care professionals regularly attend seminars and symposia arranged by 3M for their education in new techniques.

"Hands-on" training at the customer's doorstep is sometimes possible, as with a custom-built demonstration van touring the United States to acquaint telephone companies with a new 3M modular splicing system.

The opportunities that exist in the growing service sector of the economy—beyond products and commodities—have frequently been stressed by Walter S. Meyers, who became marketing vice president after two decades in charge of a 3M subsidiary which was essentially a service to advertisers.

Meyers is quick to acknowledge that marketing isn't everything, but he also reminds sales people that they are the final link between 3M and its customers.

During 3M's 75th anniversary, the growing market-orientation of the company's businesses was signalled in the creation of a ninth major operating group devoted to consumer products from a number of plants and laboratories.

Establishment of the new Consumer Products group, according to the man named to head it, Ernest B. Moffet, will bring 3M's technological and marketing resources to bear even better on specific needs of people.

"Specialization of this kind," he said, "will improve our understanding of the marketplace and help us define better the needs that exist. We expect the new setup to help other groups because it permits them to concentrate on what they are doing without a retail diversion."

Listening to learn what people need has often been more than half the battle.

Max Tyler, marketing director, Industrial Specialties division, recalls the case of Alex Kunevicius, a car salesman who came to 3M in 1966 with his idea for protecting new cars from parking-lot bumps and scratches. Kunevicius started his Custom Trim Company in a small garage, using 3M neoprene foam, and became the world's largest manufacturer of pressure-sensitive, autobody side moldings.

A one-man operator in Florida, designing and making custom hunting knives, was impressed with the service he received when he sought help in polishing his blades.

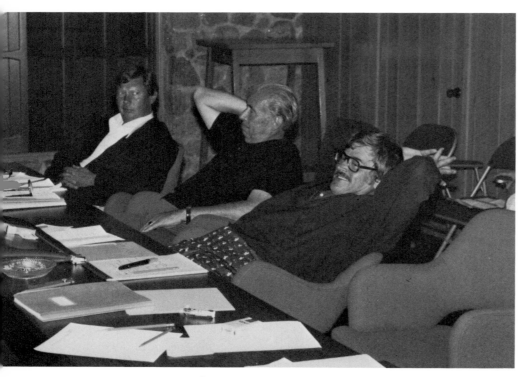

Distributor relations are part of the marketing effort. In this informal work session with a dealer advisory council are regional sales managers Bob H. Cole and Willard P. Erickson, with vice president Ernest B. Moffet, Jr.

"3M deserves a standing ovation for its care and concern for a small nobody like me," he wrote. "Your advice and suggestions have made my shop much more efficient. My knives are better, not only because of my skill but also because of your abrasive belts.

"I am a satisfied customer."

The makers and marketers at 3M had achieved the goal of all their work and planning: customer satisfaction.

The collaboration between marketing, manufacturing and technical people at 3M is evident in the planning stages as well as in the execution of a division's business plan.

Marketing strategy can include such matters as planned entry into new markets, timetables for product introductions, upcoming advertising and sales promotion campaigns, proposed pricing and the effect of price variations.

Concurrent manufacturing strategy must cover present

"Up is a nice place to be"·was the theme of a 1971 program for dental products sales representatives. Winner Ken Flaherty of California collects one of his prizes: a February flight by balloon over snow-covered Minnesota.

A 1945 ad tells war-weary consumers that their wait for "Scotch" brand tape will soon be over.

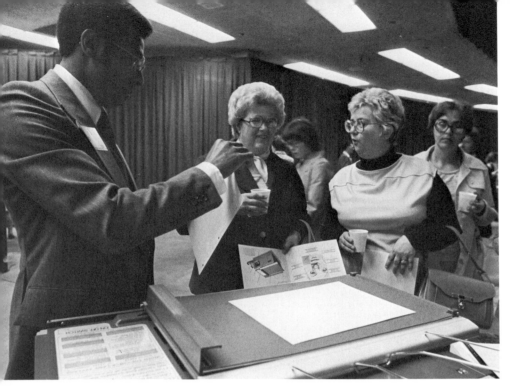

Sales development coordinator Robert A. Gregory, Duplicating Products division, collects an audience.

and future production capacity, plant expansion and new equipment needs, raw materials availability and projections of their cost, and future opportunities for process improvements.

Technical strategy adds information on product development and improvement, innovations in the markets being served, new laws, new consumer concerns.

"Business planning, to be effective," says Donald E. Garretson, vice president, finance, "must mobilize all the forces which will be called upon to administer or carry out the plan once it is made and approved.

"Planning makes people think—about goals and about problems. It starts them talking, sharing ideas, communicating goals. It makes them stand back from today's routine tasks to take a hard look at longer-range goals and problems.

"Not the least important," Garretson adds, "it helps individuals see their work assignments more clearly. The input received from all levels of our organization,

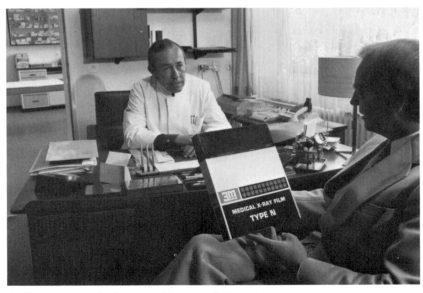

Calling on a radiologist in Europe: "Listening is even more important when we don't have the product someone needs."

Marketers with related product lines help each other. Mike Barker, center, sales supervisor in the Electro-Products division, won "Man of the Year" honors from the Hardware-Paint Trades division for his field support, as here with hardware sales representative Dave Lofstrom, left.

Industrial abrasives salesman Ricardo L. Esguerra, third from left,
receives symbolic plaque as 1974 "Sales Rep of the Year" in 3M Philippines.
With him are J. A. Buenconsejo, marketing director; G. L. Hegg, area
vice president; R. B. Valera, group sales and marketing manager.

wherever the work is done, is of tremendous value in setting or reappraising the goals realistically."

In telling how manufacturing and marketing plans are made three to five years in advance and constantly reviewed and modified, he stresses that at 3M planning "is not a guess as to what will happen, but a decision about what we want to happen and, especially, about how we will go about making it happen."

The management role in putting everything together for an operating unit at 3M was the subject of admiring comment in a 1971 best seller, "Corporation Man."

Author Antony Jay, called one of the most imaginative management consultants in Britain, was attempting an anthropological look at the structure and workings of modern corporations. He singled out two companies, 3M of America and the Marks and Spencer department store chain of Britain, as model firms.

He told of becoming interested in 3M because of a saucepan scourer: "If a firm so large and successful was bothering to launch a new saucepan scourer, it must surely be very good (which it was)." On investigating, he found an organization with almost as many products as people and he concluded that the tremendous diversity was possible only because of dedication to a principle of forming new groups and allowing them to expand whenever they could link a new product with a growth market.

Recognizing that relevance to the changing needs of people is essential to an organization's survival and continuing success, 3M leaders have often stressed the development and marketing of new, high quality products compatible with society's demands.

As many as 15 specialized staffs, ranging from toxicologists to operations analysts, stand ready to help 3M makers and marketers in their pursuit of such relevance. Technical feasibility is only one of many considerations, though certainly an important one . . . and one where 3M scientists are well equipped to help. □

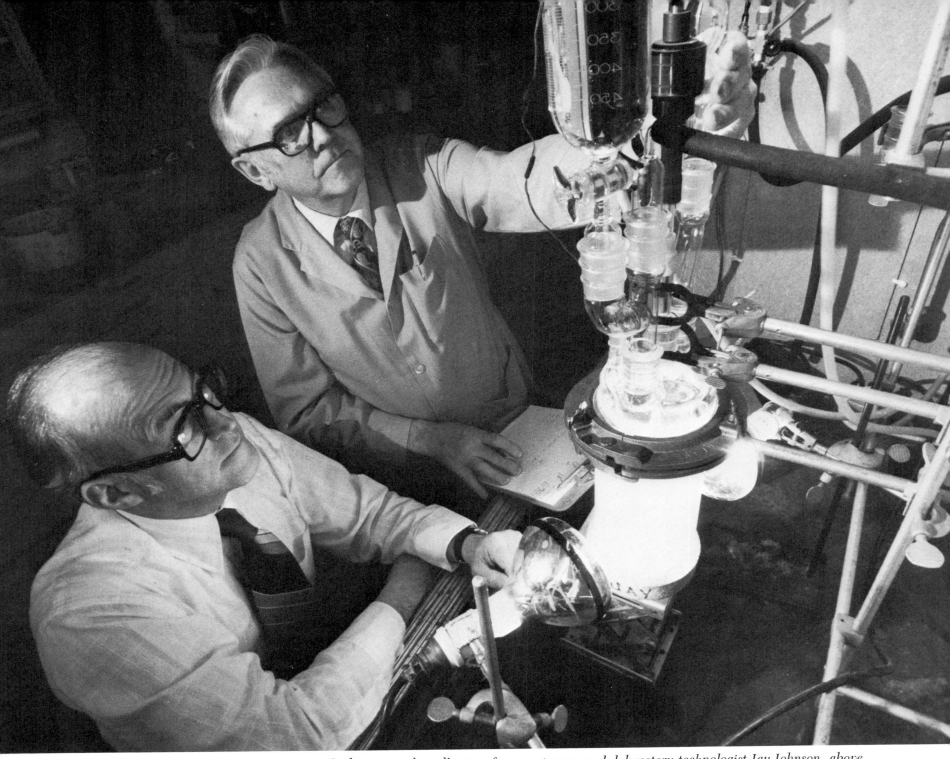

Seeking specialty adhesives for a customer need: laboratory technologist Jay Johnson, above, and corporate scientist Francis W. Brown of the Chemical Resources division.

Discovery people in action

An early quest for quality leads to scientific excellence, and researchers close to the marketplace of human needs

It was this little wooden enclosure. It was about 6 feet that way and 11 feet this way. It had shelves on one end. It had two outside windows and the kind of storm-shed door that opened up. Nothing fancy, just made out of boards and slats."

This was 3M Company's first laboratory, established in 1916 for the princely sum of $500, and described by its first full-time technical employee, William Vievering.

"There was some power cable that came from the shipping room, which supplied electricity for abrasive rub tests," Vievering says. "We used it until we got a separate motor in the laboratory."

The cubicle was so small, Vievering recalls, "that I had to back out when Mr. McKnight wanted to come in, or he had to back out when I wanted to go in."

The laboratory, however, made an immediate contribution to product quality, and 3M—which had taken 14 years to establish its first lab—set up the second within another year, at the end of 1917. This was one story above the old laboratory, larger and better.

That was the beginning of technology at 3M.

Technology grew, and Vievering along with it until his contributions earned him membership in the Carlton Society, an honor group formed in 1963 by the technical directors in charge of 3M laboratories to recognize outstanding contributors and their consistently high standards of originality, dedication and integrity in technical work. The society is named for former president

Richard P. Carlton, who realized as early as 1925 that 3M had outgrown its "rule of thumb" origins.

What began as a quest for quality in one product line has grown to include an assembly of technical talent which could staff science departments at several good-sized universities. Many in 3M research have had earlier academic careers and some continue to combine part-time teaching and campus lectures with their purposeful pursuit of industrial research, close to the marketplace of human needs.

The humble beginnings and a few early examples of bumbling serendipity or lucky happenstance make for colorful reading. But to offer them as substantially representative of industrial research activity would be like comparing 3M's web-process, precision coating expertise to sandwich-making, or like referring to a rubber stamp and ink-pad as a duplicating machine.

In more recent years, company researchers often found themselves trading thoughts with visitors of renown: space scientist Wernher von Braun, physicist Edward Teller, Nobel prize-winner Linus Pauling, telecommunications pioneer Peter Goldmark and Atomic Energy Commission chairman Dixy Lee Ray.

An invitation to think big and positively in a cross-disciplinary way, issued by R. Buckminster Fuller during a 1972 lecture at 3M, was well received, with good reason.

The futuristic inventor was appearing as final guest in a

year-long series of programs for the 3M Technical Forum, formed by 3M scientists 20 years earlier for the express purpose of encouraging a free and active interchange of information and the cross-fertilization of ideas among company researchers.

Fuller stressed that technical people can play a great role in a changing world, especially if they capitalize on the relationships between technical specialties.

"Even the long-standing lines of distinction between the animate and the inanimate are becoming blurred, as in bio-chemistry," he noted.

The famed inventor of the geodesic dome agreed with his audience that through intelligent use of technology man can do more with less, and raise the world's standard of living.

Fuller differed with those who set arbitrary limits to growth, based on obsolete physical accounting methods. Older ways of measuring wealth, resources and potential, he said, offer no adequate way of dealing with the metaphysical, the transcendental and the uniquely human ability to modify tools and control the regeneration of the physical universe.

His hour and a half discourse without notes earned him a standing ovation from 3M's technical community. He accepted the applause "as a cheer for truth . . . nothing personal."

Formal development activities began in the 1920s, and the first Central Research laboratory was formed in 1937. This early technological spadework led to a product harvest in the 1950s, described by Dr. Robert M. Adams, vice president of research and development, as "a kind of golden era of results."

He explained: "In the '50s, we saw the commercialization of reflective products, printing products, copying products, fluorochemicals, electrical tapes, magnetic tape and many, many others.

"And many of the things that have happened in the '60s and '70s have been innovations on those things or have been developments which came out of them."

All this, Adams says, has given 3M "a reputation—a very nice reputation—as an innovator . . . of coming up with interesting new products." This view was endorsed by *Dun's Review* magazine in 1963, when it picked 3M as "one of the 10 best-managed companies in the country."

The magazine said, "Minnesota Mining's genius lies in the way it has contrived to tame R&D, that most volatile and elusive, ruinous or rewarding of corporate activities, so that it produces an orderly, constant stream of results.

"In harnessing R&D, the company still permits, and indeed, encourages, a substantial amount of experimental 'doodling.' At 3M, management believes that the mixing of these ingredients carries with it a guarantee of future successes."

These "future successes" are a concern of nearly 5,000 men and women working in some 60 company laboratories worldwide. The quest continues. In 1976, the company spent $158 million for research and

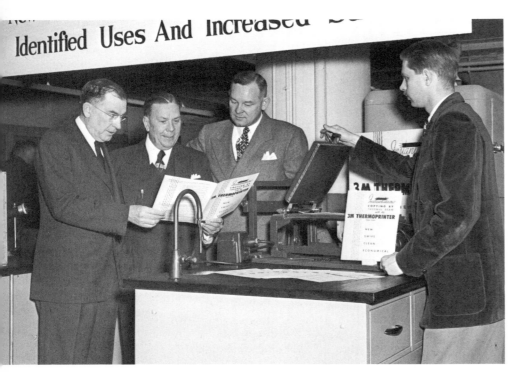

Bryce L. Clark, right, previews the "Thermo-Fax" copier in 1949 for, from left, McKnight, Carlton, Charles W. Walton.

development, 4.5 percent of worldwide sales.

"According to the best measurements that we have, about 22 percent of these sales were from products that were not in the line five years previously," Adams says.

Developing these saleable new products is an example of how 3M "continues its growth and success by treating human problems as business opportunities," Adams says.

He offered a few safeguards against technological obsolescence—or unemployment for short:

"If you continually come up with products and services that people will want and need in the future, you ensure your relevance, and your commercial success. Nobody succeeds by offering superfluous or irrelevant systems— or by offering today's products to tomorrow's world."

Trying to find new or better ways to solve human problems has provided a common impetus to 3M's research and development program from its very beginnings. It implies a risk element and provides what Dr. Charles W. Walton, retired R&D vice president, once called "the spice we need . . . excitement" to produce extraordinary results.

This spice, he said, is "primarily people excitement, which can be converted into product excitement, which, in turn, results in market excitement.

"Without these forms of excitement, little enthusiasm or spark is generated in the business engine, and little or no real success can be achieved."

Walton cited an example "where, in one instance, the excitement chain was complete, and the product was a success.

"Our people had long recognized the need for a presensitized metal plate for use in offset lithography. Our first effort to develop such a product lasted two years and ended in technical failure.

"One year later, a new team of people reactivated the project to try some new ideas based on recently developed technology. Even with this new technology, they found they still did not have the key to the problem. Again, the project was officially shelved.

"Thirty days later, one of the people who had been frustrated by both failures but who was still excited by the product concept, wanted to try still another new idea.

John M. Case, left, and Clifford L. Jewett,
co-inventors of metal presensitized litho plate.
Their invention set the standard for
the worldwide offset printing industry.

Expanding on a technology; magnetic tape for television

"This idea produced at low cost the first product of its kind to enter the market. Customers quickly purchased the printing plate, because it performed well and saved them both time and money. It created considerable market excitement—and it fulfilled hopes and dreams."

Another word which applies to 3M technology is synergism; one thing combines with another, and the result often is greater than the sum of the parts.

For example, film was a basic ingredient in most of the different tapes 3M began coating. It was logical for 3M to develop its own film technology to assure itself a reliable supply.

New-product introductions thus soon expanded to include a diversity of items such as photographic films, graphic-arts films, X-ray films, overhead-projection transparencies and microfilms.

In developing precision-coating technology for producing high-quality coated abrasives and the early tapes, the company became expert in manufacturing the adhesives used in them, too. Consequently, an extensive rubber and resin technology developed.

Since 3M made adhesives for its own use, it was natural to make them for others as well. As with masking tape, the car industry was the first to be served. In switching from wooden to all-steel car bodies, manufacturers needed new methods of attaching upholstery and trim to the inside of their vehicles. Adhesives were required which would hold fabric to steel but would not be absorbed and cause stains. 3M rubber and resin technology produced such adhesives.

The first bulk adhesive sale went to an automaker in 1931 to fasten rubber mats to running boards. Since then, that original product has multiplied into more than 1,500 formulations of adhesives, coatings and sealers—in liquid, solid, paste and film forms. They're widely used now by the aerospace, marine, construction and general industrial fields—in addition to the car industry—for joining, sealing and protecting just about every type of material imaginable.

When 3Mers developed an adhesive that would stick to vinyl, the result was a new and better electrical tape,

Splicing with the first vinyl electrical tape: "Scotch" Number 33.

which in turn led to formation of an Electrical Products group serving worldwide markets with insulation, telecommunications and electronic products.

Looking beyond 3M's tape and adhesives capabilities to other needs in communications and energy transmission, a young electro-mechanical engineer, E. Wayne Bollmeier, helped invent "Scotchlok" connectors and an improved connector for the telephone industry. Further refinements by the time of 3M's 75th anniversary gave Bollmeier, as electrical products group vice president, the satisfaction of seeing an extension of his original "Minnesota connection" serving the people of Malaysia in their all new telephone system.

Magnetic tapes also were being perfected, combining 3M's own technologies with careful study of two German Magnetophon recorders and a supply of recording tape obtained at the end of World War II by John T. Mullin, who had been a Signal Corps officer.

In 1947, an American firm, Brush Development Co., marketed an amateur sound-recording machine, and 3M introduced the first commercially acceptable magnetic recording tape—"Scotch" No. 100 magnetic tape. It consisted of a black iron oxide coating on a paper backing.

Within a year, 3M introduced "Scotch" No. 111 magnetic tape, which utilized red iron oxide on an acetate backing to produce superior audio fidelity.

A few years later, two magnetic tape researchers found themselves working on a product to record pictures as well as sound. A note of urgency was added to their earlier efforts when 3M learned that the Ampex Corp. the next day would introduce the world's first broadcast video recorder. Several tapes were to be played on the machine, but none from 3M.

Working from 2:30 p.m. until the next morning, Mel Sater and Joe Mazzitello prepared a magnetic tape on which an image could be recorded for playback. Production workers coated and slit the product, which employed an experimental binder. The company had no two-inch reels to wind the tape on, so cores were cut with a hacksaw.

In the morning, the tapes were flown to Chicago for the

recorder introduction and were declared to be of superior quality. This "overnight success" story helped to establish 3M as a leader in video recording.

Carl S. Miller was a Canadian-born graduate student in physics at the University of Minnesota in the late 1930s when he developed a strong dislike for copying library materials as he grew tired of writer's cramp.

Miller, with a new Ph.D., joined 3M in 1940 and began work on differential absorption (a dark object absorbs more heat than a light object). Watching a brown leaf melt into a snowbank, Miller mentally noted that this was an example of differential absorption of heat from the sun. He also began to wonder whether the principle could be applied to copy a written image.

Like the leaf melting into snow, a dark image would absorb more heat than the paper on which it appeared. Could the image, therefore, be transferred onto a heat-sensitive paper?

It took Miller and 3M a decade and a million dollars, but he answered his question by developing the world's first dry copying system, the "Thermo-Fax" copying machines.

A Duplicating Products division was born. It, in turn, began to spawn additional, image-related products—microfilm, overhead-projection transparencies, carbonless papers, facsimile-transmission and word-processing equipment.

The technical synergism led from creation of one product division to an entire Graphic Systems group, comprised of four divisions, a department and its own nationwide sales and service organization for office-information systems, 3M Business Products Sales Inc. (BPSI, pronounced "Bipsee" by many).

The Graphic Systems group produced sales which, in 1976, were 21 percent of 3M's worldwide total.

A production manager for lithographic printing plates, Ray Herzog, joined Duplicating Products as coordinator of the "Thermo-Fax" project and became, in succession, division and group vice president, 3M president and, in 1975, chairman and chief executive officer.

It is axiomatic at 3M that "to earn the opportunity for

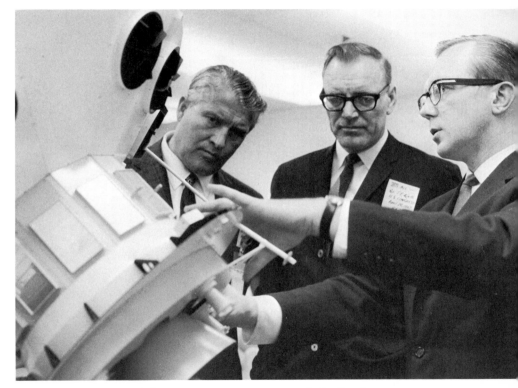

Wernher von Braun, left, U.S. Congressman Joseph E. Karth, center, with R. Lee Sisler during 1967 visit to 3M.

John T. Mullin, above left, who introduced magnetic tape to the U.S., and S. Lee Pastor, early designer of tape recorders, examine a cassette recorder. Right, echo-free environment in 3M Central Research, for testing recorders, tapes, related products.

A possible product to make textiles stain-resistant?

great reward normally requires the undertaking of great risk." This perhaps is most evident in one of the largest and most expensive research programs in the company's history.

This adventure began in 1944 when 3M purchased the rights to a process for producing fluorochemical compounds. The company at first could make only low-boiling fluorocarbon gases and inert fluorochemical liquids. No commercial markets were known or could be found. The process was so new, and the materials it produced were so unusual, however, that the technology aroused great excitement among researchers.

But after several years of experimentation, neither uses nor customers had been found. This led to an examination of byproducts, some of which turned out to be reactive, fluorine-containing materials.

There were no uses for these products either, but as Walton noted, "They surely were different, not only in their properties, but also in cost. They were just about the most expensive organic chemicals known to man," at about $40 a pound.

One day, a laboratory associate spilled a sample of the material on her tennis shoes. The substance resisted attempts to wash it off with water or hydrocarbon solvents. Furthermore, the affected area of her tennis shoes resisted soiling.

The lab associate saw this as a bothersome clean-up problem, but chemists Patsy Sherman and Sam Smith viewed it differently. They saw it as a possible product to make textiles resist water and oil stains.

They worked to enhance the liquid repellency of the compound and to reduce its cost. Their product was introduced in 1956 as "Scotchgard" fabric protector. In 3M's 75th anniversary year, there were nearly 30 formula variations for "Scotchgard" products for protecting materials ranging from furniture fabrics to wall coverings and luggage to carpets.

A broad range of fluorochemical industrial products also has been developed for making paint and floor waxes spread evenly and dry smoothly, for cooling laser beams and for treating paper packaging to prevent oil and grease from penetrating.

The technology has become a major strength of the Commercial Chemicals division.

Fluorochemicals are an example of what Richard P. Carlton meant when he said that the company, indeed, has stumbled onto some of its new products, but "you can't stumble if you're not in motion."

Researchers were in motion, searching for a new backing material for electrical-insulation tapes during the early 1940s. They experimented with synthetic fibers mixed with wood pulp. But the construction wasn't strong, nor could it be produced in uniform thickness.

The experimenters shifted to synthetic fibers carded on a textile loom, and a crude process of "dry" papermaking was perfected. Perhaps those synthetic fibers could be bonded to produce a useful nonwoven product.

The technology, however, was a three-time loser. This worried researcher Alvin W. Boese considerably and repeatedly. On the Friday after Thanksgiving in 1947, again in 1948, and finally in 1949, the recommendation had been made to scuttle his project. The date was selected purposefully and tactfully, "so as not to ruin my turkey dinner," Boese says.

After the third adverse recommendation, he adds, "I couldn't imagine that we'd get a fourth chance." But it came in the form of a three-month reprieve in which to develop something useful and marketable.

The material was not strong, and it was lackluster in appearance; those were the problems. Lamination of lustrous fibers onto a nonwoven web had to be the last-resort answer, or the axe would fall, Boese thought.

He got a dimestore comb, 40 ten-cent sewing-machine bobbins and a cone of acetate yarn. "We wound the fiber and pulled it through the comb," Boese says. "We laid the yarn shoulder to shoulder on top of the web. It worked like a dream, the 40 bobbins and comb producing a ribbon about 3/8-inch wide. We could have carried the process right into production the next day," Boese recalls.

By June, Boese and his fellow workers had built a piece of equipment which could produce a decorative ribbon 12 inches wide. They learned more about dyeing and resin coating and were ready to go.

"In August, we said we'd make 25,000 yards for test sale

A tangled web, a fine-tooth comb, a budding business

for Christmas," Boese says. By mid-October, a quarter-million yards of ribbon had been sold, and the market had been established.

Nonwovens have since formed the basis for a variety of 3M products ranging from "Scotch-Brite" cleaning and finishing materials to surgical and protective face masks. The technology was unusual, because it didn't relate to a specific product area of its own, Boese said. Any variant might go "to a different division where you would lose sight of it when someone else picked up the ball."

For example, the early backbone of 3M's health-care product line was a nonwoven surgical tape that "breathed" and had a chemically inert adhesive which caused no allergies or irritation. A Health Care Products and Services group evolved and, in 1976, produced 7 percent of all 3M worldwide sales.

It is estimated that products from nonwoven technology annually produce more sales than all of 3M had in any of its first 50 years. But not every one was a commercial success.

About $10,000 was spent on a machine to make nonwoven brassiere cups that were cheaper and stronger than their sewn counterparts. "We had a bona-fide substance," Boese says, "but the textile companies each wanted an exclusive, which it was 3M policy not to grant."

Laboratory personnel work on pilot-stage development of nonwoven fabrics in 1946.

While interest waned in the brassiere cup, the technology did produce various face masks. Thus while research does not always produce what one is looking for, very often it produces other things of equal or greater value.

Reflective sheeting is another laboratory idea which has been multiplied and modified to become a major presence in transportation, safety, identification and decorative markets. Again, the product line's success belies its shaky beginning and precarious survival as a fledgling technology.

Costs were high, and 3M's first reflective product, a roadway center striping, was neither adequately reflective nor able to withstand the rigors of traffic or weather.

Another neophyte product for street and highway signs wasn't any better than the roadway striping. The glimmer in 3M's eye for this new technology faded, and the obituary was written.

Philip V. Palmquist, technical director of the Special Enterprises department and a pioneer in reflective technology, recalls, "Management finally lost faith in what really was a poor product and told me one day in 1938 to stop working on reflective sheeting. I was ordered back to coated abrasives . . . a project where anything you did in technical effort resulted in immediate dollars."

Palmquist wasn't married at the time and "nobody was around to stop me from doing it," so he returned to the laboratory from 7 to 11 p.m. about four nights a week to work on reflective sheeting. He developed a product 100 times brighter than white paint and about 30 times brighter than previous 3M reflective materials. Management became interested in the product again.

In the decade following 1938 "Scotchlite" technology was developed and began to reflect just about everything 3M wanted but a profit. A major problem was overcome when Palmquist sparked invention of a process to enclose the reflective beads behind a plastic film. This "Flat Top" construction, as it's called, eliminated a tendency for the product not to reflect properly when dirty or wet.

As new-product manager at the time, Bert Cross was a leading risk-taker and champion for the profitless product. Tenaciously, he kept the development progressing.

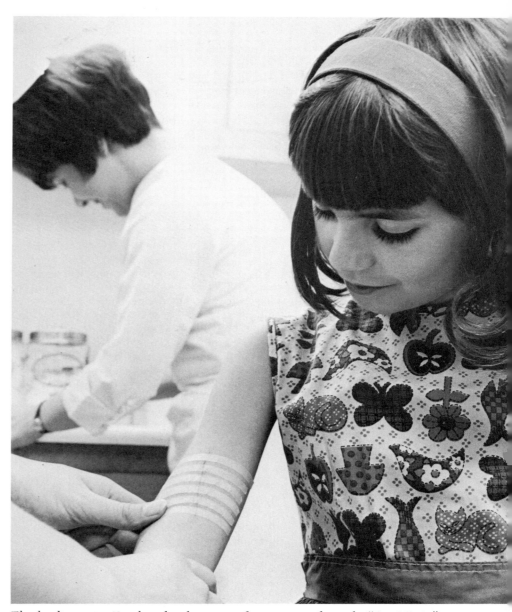

The healing arts: Further development of nonwovens brought "Steri-Strip" closures so that surgeons could repair some surgical incisions and accidental wounds without the trauma of stitch removal.

Academy award, and an encore

The telephone rang just before Christmas 1968, and the caller from Hollywood told Phil Palmquist, "You've been nominated for an award for a major technical contribution."

"I didn't know what they were talking about," Palmquist said. "It finally got through that I might receive an Oscar."

And he did — for developing a front-projection screen which is used to provide realistic backdrop scenery for motion pictures. (Only 17 such technical awards have been given in 45 years. An earlier winner had been CinemaScope.)

Previously, filmmakers used a rear-projection backdrop which limited them to a 14-foot screen in a dark room. Actors were off screen if they took 10 paces; the scenery looked fake, and there were myriad problems with lighting and images.

Palmquist's front-projection screen was based on "Scotchlite" retroreflective technology. The concept eliminated using a dark building and permitted building backdrop screens as big as 40 feet high and 100 feet wide. The first major movie to use the method was "2001: A Space Odyssey."

At the 1969 Academy Award presentations, Palmquist's wife said, "Gee, Phil, this is exciting. Do it again." So, Palmquist investigated and found that Hollywood had another vexing and costly problem. Blood-drenched costumes had to be cleaned between retakes of scenes. This idled expensive film crews.

"We devised a substance incorporating red microspheres held in a thickener. It looked and functioned as blood did, but it 'sat' right on the surface of the clothing and washed right off," Palmquist said. That's 3M's "Nextel" blood, hardly a major product, he admits.

"I received a citation for that. It wasn't an Oscar, but my wife did get to the Academy Awards and the Academy Ball a second time."

"Would you believe," he recalls, "that it took us eight long, dry years to finally make five cents in 'Scotchlite' profits—or at least to get the bookkeepers to agree that we made some money." Initial sales were $3,500 in the first year; $10,500 in the second; $16,000 in the third year, and $33,000 in the fourth.

During World War II, sale of "Scotchlite" material began to increase, paced by military orders. Among other things, "Scotchlite" sheeting was used for blackout markings on aircraft landing strips and along tank trails.

After the war, during the recovery and expansion of civilian transportation, the uses and sales of "Scotchlite" products began to multiply.

Reflectivity not only became accepted as desirable but was considered by many to be necessary for a variety of safety and identification purposes—including license plates and traffic markings. Corporate identity and advertising materials for trucks, buses and aircraft followed, along with decorative accenting of automobiles.

The grow and divide syndrome was working again. A formerly profitless capsule technology had spawned a family tree of myriad products, which branched out in many directions. (See chart, page 112)

From a small development project there eventually emerged one of 3M's largest product groups, including four units related to reflective technology—Traffic Control Materials division, Safety Systems division, Decorative Products division and Traffic Control Devices department. Cross became president and then chairman of 3M, followed in those positions by Harry Heltzer, another "Scotchlite" pioneer.

Looking back from retirement, Heltzer says, "I don't think we fully appreciated that 'Scotchlite' products represented such a high level of technology—until after the basic patent ran out.

"In the early days, others were able to make swatches of reflective material that looked pretty good, but nobody was able to produce it yard after yard and have the optical properties, the durability and the handling properties of 'Scotchlite' products."

Keeping technically in tune with the needs of people is what the Photographic Products division has done with its

Nucleus of the "Scotchlite" project in 1943 photo. From left, Donald J. Douglas, Edward P. Davis, Bert S. Cross, Robert L. Ackerberg, Paul M. Magoon, Philip V. Palmquist and Harry Heltzer. Not shown: Donald O. Opstad

medical X-ray films, which were greeted as a significant advance in the "state of the art" by technicians and doctors who use them.

The Trimax Micro Dosage Imaging System, for example, uses a high-speed film which cuts down exposure time. It allows a radiologist to take stop-action X-rays, which are not blurred by motion, and it reduces radiation exposure for the patient by as much as eight times.

These Trimax films are combined with a phosphor intensifying screen to permit reading X-rays at higher levels of magnification to improve radiological examinations.

Another breakthrough was achieved with the 3M High Light System, which eliminates need for a darkroom in which to load and process X-ray film. The radiologist can remain with the patient at all times, decreasing the chance of accidents. Expensive, cumbersome X-ray film holders are eliminated.

"The key to research" and technical successes such as these, Heltzer once reminded an audience of 3M scientists, "is that people—not dollars—develop new products and new technologies.

"So, when we say that we are spending more than a hundred million dollars on research and development, we're really betting on our people and on the qualities that enable them to develop new and improved ideas, such as the ability to fire the imagination of their associates and stimulate output by others."

The technical people of whom Heltzer spoke form a catalyst which causes a reaction between inspiration and perspiration that produces significant advances in technology. The success of former researchers depended as much upon their personal traits as on test tubes.

Intuition—A. E. (Tim) Raymond, pioneer in improving coated abrasives, "had the feeling that probably abrasives were like a sharp skate—that, on a warm day, you could cut farther into the ice with the same sharp skate than you could on a cold day.

"Thinking about that . . . maybe through heat induction we could allow a metal to be cut faster. We first tried by using a torch on brass. After it got to a certain temperature, we could cut it like putty, and then we went into tungsten and raised the temperature higher and higher until we found out what temperature we had to have to make that thing melt or cut.

"I turned the research over to the Abrasives division, where it was perfected and applied to solve problems."

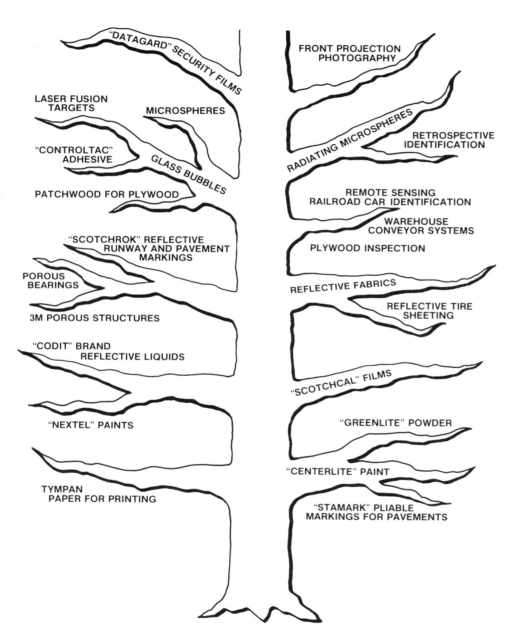

"DATAGARD" SECURITY FILMS

LASER FUSION TARGETS

MICROSPHERES

"CONTROLTAC" ADHESIVE

GLASS BUBBLES

PATCHWOOD FOR PLYWOOD

"SCOTCHROK" REFLECTIVE RUNWAY AND PAVEMENT MARKINGS

POROUS BEARINGS

3M POROUS STRUCTURES

"CODIT" BRAND REFLECTIVE LIQUIDS

"NEXTEL" PAINTS

TYMPAN PAPER FOR PRINTING

FRONT PROJECTION PHOTOGRAPHY

RADIATING MICROSPHERES

RETROSPECTIVE IDENTIFICATION

REMOTE SENSING RAILROAD CAR IDENTIFICATION

WAREHOUSE CONVEYOR SYSTEMS

PLYWOOD INSPECTION

REFLECTIVE FABRICS

REFLECTIVE TIRE SHEETING

"SCOTCHCAL" FILMS

"GREENLITE" POWDER

"CENTERLITE" PAINT

"STAMARK" PLIABLE MARKINGS FOR PAVEMENTS

From the basic "Scotchlite" brand reflective sheeting technology, a family of related products and services.

Brighter and safer roofs for the home-builder: Howard Boxmeyer, right, and a customer check out roofing granules.

Practicality—In 1930, 3M acquired Wausau Abrasives Company, which owned Rib Mountain, a massive mound of quartzite. A challenge was issued, "Find a profitable use for our new mountain."

George Swenson and Clifford Jewett developed a process for ceramically applying color coatings to roofing-shingle granules, an advance long desired by the roofing industry. Jewett also developed a process which reduced coating costs by two-thirds and expanded color capabilities.

Rib Mountain, for a time, was the "Big Rock Candy Mountain" for 3M; it put the company into a significant new business—and produced a handsome profit.

Quartzite later was replaced by a better mineral for roofing granules, but Rib Mountain remains in use. Forty acres of the land were donated to the city of Wausau, Wis., for parks and skiing.

Leadership and foresight—Richard P. Carlton, supplied organization and direction to 3M technology beginning in the 1920s and eventually became president of the company.

As Tim Raymond said of Carlton: "He had the ability of

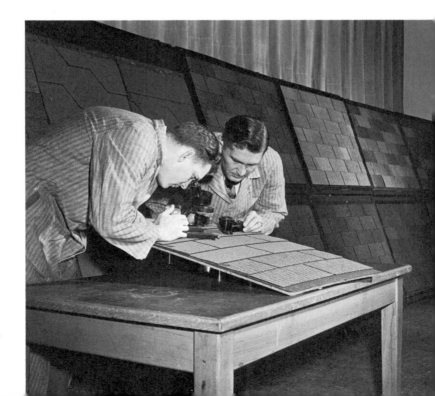

The Carlton Society was formed in 1963 to recognize extraordinary scientific and technical contributions to the company. Charter members were, from left: Front row, George W. Swenson, Henry N. Stephens, Bert S. Cross, Leonard R. Nestor, Richard G. Drew and Francis G. Okie; back row, Cyril P. Pesek, accepting the honor for the late E. M. Johnson, Hubert J. Tierney, George P. Netherly, A. E. (Tim) Raymond, Clifford L. Jewett, Joseph H. Kugler, E. Waldo Kellgren, Lloyd A. Hatch and Harvey J. Livermore.

analyzing new things, new developments, and he'd support those things, because he was very sharp at telling whether something was going to work or whether it wouldn't work.

"He had dreams of research . . . and could foresee the need of research not only to control but also to develop. Not only that, but the need to have a research group of technical people who could expand anything that might develop."

In the 1920s and '30s, Carlton summed up a complex philosophy quite simply, according to Raymond: "He said

that if you get an idea and the idea is basically new, if you can coat it on 3M equipment in an efficient way to meet a demonstrable need, then you've probably got something worthwhile."

Before he joined 3M, George P. Netherly, another pioneer in abrasives, had worked for a firm where "all the thinking was done and written down in a little book, and you went by the book or else. They said you have one more privilege than a soldier. A soldier can't quit."

"So I said [upon arriving at 3M], Mr. Carlton, do you have a list of rules for employees that I ought to be

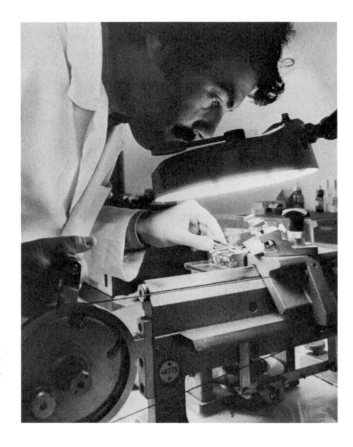

*Research in Italy:
Alfio Chiarlone
conducts film test*

studying over the weekend?' 'No, we don't have any rules, you're old enough to know what ought to be done,' Carlton said.

"It was kind of a free-wheeling outfit. Carlton wanted results."

Innovation—Harry Heltzer, experimenting, made glass spheres "by pouring molten glass on the floor, letting it bounce, and then picking up the little beads."

Then came a slightly improved methodology. "One of our first laboratory attempts was to melt about a cupful of glass in a crucible and pour the molten glass out of the sixth floor window of the Mineral Building. As the glass fell through the air, some would form droplets, solidify, and become spherical in shape. We would sweep them off the cemented area," Heltzer recalls.

Technology has become more sophisticated and the personnel have changed, but apparently not the personalities. Dr. Hugh G. Bryce, vice president of Central Research, notes that:

"Management of research at 3M is not a very difficult thing, because it is mostly taking good people, stimulating them to get involved with something that challenges them and giving some guidance as to which way is most likely to meet their goal of achieving whatever success means to them."

Central Research Laboratories employs more than 400 technical persons who have three avenues of advancement according to Bryce: "To become an outstanding technologist; to fly off with a new-product opportunity to an operating division; or to become an administrator."

Dr. Robert Adams finds in 3M research a natural tendency to apply technology practically.

"If somebody starts what we call a basic research project," he says, ". . . sooner or later, he's going to ask himself to do a little dreaming. How can what you're doing be turned into some sort of technology which will promise products and processes that someone somewhere will find useful."

Central Research and division laboratories are as two prongs on a technological tuning fork. They vibrate intellectually, and in harmony.

"Divisions, of course, are concerned with the research and technology of their particular products," Bryce notes. "If they want to draw on us (Central Research) for our sophisticated expertise, they do.

"For instance, a tape division might need a different kind of tape with a different adhesive. They might come to us and ask, 'Do you people have a different kind of adhesive,' because they'll be familiar with their own technologies. And they know we have some people who are dealing with rather new kinds of chemistry and might be able to generate that adhesive."

Bryce also speaks to the need for scientists to be multilingual in the lexicon of marketing, manufacturing and management. The person who can do this, he says, becomes the link between abstract theory and concrete need.

George Netherly said he believed that 3M "has gotten more new products when somebody recognized a market and said, 'Now can you make something that will do this,' than when we have searched until we found something and said, 'Can you find a use for this? Where can we sell it?' "

Netherly's comment and the earlier thoughts of the visiting Buckminster Fuller are reinforced by a later visitor, who seemed to recognize 3M as a leader in meeting the needs of the marketplace.

Dennis Meadows, chief author of a book, "The Limits to Growth," addressed 3M's technical community in 1974: "If I were addressing others, it might be a little more difficult for me to urge an increase in research. But here in this company it seems to me a growth rate in research is a very appropriate activity . . . I must say with a good deal of genuine admiration, 3M has done a much more significant job of coping with [the bigness] aspect of growth than any other large company I am familiar with."

3M's first laboratory, the "little wooden enclosure . . . about 6 feet that way and 11 feet this way," has burgeoned into a sophisticated technical organization; specialists today abound where a few intuitive tinkerers once pioneered alone. □

Lab technician Kathy Williams' normal body temperature brings to a boil a "Fluorinert" liquid, among many 3M fluorochemicals used in electronic testing, cooling, fabric and paper protection, and fire-fighting.

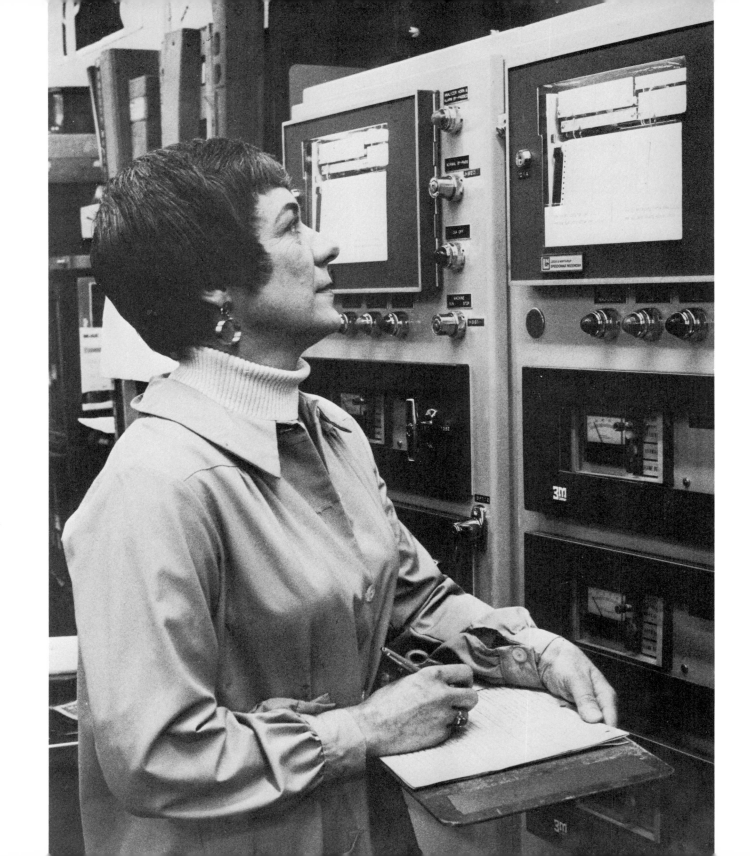

Who we are

"If I could ask for anything, it would be for good people who are determined to be successful. I guess maybe I'm lucky, because it seems to me we've got them." –R. H. Herzog, 1975

On June 23, 1977, Eileen Dodge of Birmingham, Michigan, read about 3M's 75th birthday in a Detroit newspaper. The article recounted some failures and mistakes of the company whose stock in the early years was traded in Duluth bars, two shares for a shot, and noted that "The company was founded on a mistake and prospered on industrial pratfalls."

Mrs. Dodge responded with a birthday message to 3M in which she commented on the newspaper story. "I've read too many biographies," she wrote, "to be beguiled into thinking that life has been all beer, skittles and bumbling for a company that has become one of the grandest in American industry.

"This version of 3M's history is colorful, amusing and a great attention getter . . . I love a rakish sense of humor and am charmed that you powers-that-be can tolerate a gentle poke at your dignity."

Mrs. Dodge's sentiments are echoed frequently by customers, competitors—even critics—impressed with the informality of 3M people who, as one observer noted, "take their work, but not themselves, seriously."

A former member of the "powers-that-be," retired director Bob Westbee, summed it up this way: "A great asset 3M has is the ability to laugh at itself and have a good time as it goes along.

"I speak of this company as though it is a person, for in so many ways it is one large person made up of all the people in the company."

A financial analyst, visiting 3M for the first time to appraise the company's performance and prospects, carried Westbee's observation a step further. At home in the formal and traditional business environment of New York City, he was impressed with what he called the "free and easy" atmosphere at 3M.

"You are often cited as one of the best managed companies," he said, "and now I have a better idea why. Your people don't overmanage. You provide a relaxed atmosphere and good incentives. You encourage instead of nitpick.

"You're a little different from most companies."

Jim Thwaits uses "elite" in describing 3M. "I want to make it even more elite," he has observed. "I don't want 3M ever to get to be just a place for people to come to work. I want it to be a place where people have a joy in coming to work.

"You have to have great faith in people. You have to

Tape plant foreman Lorraine Maloney monitors coating oven. She started with 3M as a stock and order packer.

"Let him get his feet wet and he'll work it out."

1937 champions in St. Paul City Commercial League golf.
Standing: William Figge, Herbert Buetow, Arnold Melin, Elbert Lund
and, seated, Hubert Tierney, Clarence Sampair.

outline the tasks and the challenges and encourage them to set their eyes on the heights. Then you must be available to support and counsel, to help and advise.

"But don't," he said emphatically, "tell them how to do it. That's their job."

Charles Pflager, purchasing agent, agrees that 3M is different.

"The day I was hired," he said, "the attitude was 180 degrees different from any other job I ever went into. In other shops, I was introduced to my foreman, and he put me to work. At 3M, I was not only introduced to the foreman, I was introduced to all the supervisors; I was introduced to the people I would be working with; I was shown how I would fit into things and right off the bat I felt part of an organization. It's been that way ever since.

"I'll always be grateful to 3M that when I was asked to go into purchasing, no one came in and said, 'This is exactly how the rules go; this is exactly how you do things.' They put me in an office and respected me enough to say, 'Let him get his feet wet and he'll work it out his own way.' We are able to fly a little bit, and that little bit means an awful lot."

Pflager worked his way from a machinist position to tool-and-die maker and shop superintendent. After 17 years with 3M, he purchases tooling and optics for the corporation. "I don't think there are any stumbling blocks for those who have initiative," he said. "Lack of education can be a temporary stumbling block—that's an area that has affected me—but there's more than one way of being educated. I'm pleased that 3M usually looks past the fact that a man or woman may lack a degree, and considers intelligence and drive."

Thwaits and Pflager have never discussed the matter, but they express similar observations from widely different viewpoints. Attitude and enthusiasm bind them together with 3M men and women all over the world.

Perhaps the greatest reward for a person's work is not what a person gets for it, but what that person becomes by it.

3M encourages its people to "become" through formal and informal training programs, experience and personal initiative. Sometimes, when the course of one person's

A spin in the fun barrel and a friendly tug-of-war are often part of the merriment when employee families gather for plant or department picnics.

career is threatened, employee benefits keep things on track, and the bond of mutual respect between the individual and his company is strengthened:

Stricken with polio during his first year of employment with 3M in 1951, Walter Krueger, engineering research specialist, fought the disease more than six months, and returned on crutches to his new job.

"I have faith in 3M, which showed so much faith in me," he said. He now heads a three-man team that applies its extrusion expertise to injection molding processes, which are used to produce technical ceramics, tape dispenser cores, magnetic tape cassettes and reels and various plastic containers.

Pat Rooney, an advertising manager in 1963 in Graphic Systems, was injured in a car accident that left him a quadriplegic. Today, he travels the country, developing a telephone assistance program for 3M Business Products

*A regard for people
in times of trouble,
usually with a personal touch*

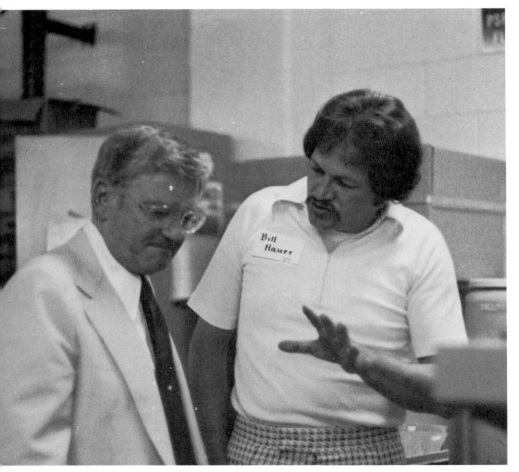

*Bill Hauer, production supervisor at a film processing station, holds
the attention of a visiting group vice president, John Pitblado.*

Centers, and serves in his "spare time" as chairman of the board of the Sister Kenny Institute. Rooney's comeback, as are many, was one in which personal determination played a large part.

A personal touch, halfway around the world from home, was added to the medical benefits of Jerold Bloom, former publications director of an accounting firm, who was stricken with Rocky Mountain spotted fever while on vacation, just seven months after joining 3M.

"I was," he said, "the first known case of the disease in Finland; so it took weeks before the doctors there could diagnose my disease. The managing director of 3M Finland stopped by to introduce himself and then visited me from time to time with words of encouragement and offers of help."

After 52 days of hospitalization in Helsinki Bloom was able to return to the United States and after an additional month and a half on partial pay through a company income maintenance plan, resume his editorial duties with 3M Public Relations.

Those manifestations of 3M regard for people are personal; sometimes the manifestation is more public:

The day shift of 4,000 employees had just reported to work at the St. Paul plant on February 8, 1951, when an explosion and fire shredded the six-story minerals building, killing 14 and injuring 51 men and women.

Business Week magazine reported, "What followed was a miracle of organization and fast thinking. Many things were done, and all at once. Evacuation, rescue, care of the injured, notification of the bereft. All with communications smashed and panic a deadly possibility."

Company officers raced to affected homes. Baby-sitters were brought so relatives could come to the injured without delay. A 3Mer was assigned to the family of each injured person — to find the best medical care, to bring in distant relatives, to make emergency loans — and where necessary make funeral arrangements or even buy cemetery plots.

In the first hour or so after the blast, one manager was heard to express concern about the customers: "This'll put us weeks behind schedule."

A man working alongside him snapped, "Let's take care

of our people first; then we'll worry about customers." That man was Herb Buetow, soon to become 3M president.

And customers, notified of their temporary relegation to second priority, responded with calls, telegrams and sacks of mail, asking if they too could do something.

"Doing something" beyond the ordinary is a long-standing tradition. In 1930 during the Depression when breadwinners stood in line for jobs at 25 cents an hour, 3M established its own pension fund and sickness and disability insurance. These programs were followed in 1932 by one of the nation's first company-paid unemployment insurance plans.

Such measures had an extraordinary effect on the morale of the 735 men and women then working for 3M. No unemployment payments ever had to be made under 3M's program, which was replaced by a federal unemployment compensation program established in 1935.

Other programs followed, each designed to go at least part of the way in easing the concerns of 3M people for the health and welfare of themselves and their families. Long after the Depression years, when jobs were plentiful, 3M people stayed with "The Mining." Jobs became careers.

Through the years, the employees in some plants have chosen to be represented by a union in their collective bargaining efforts.

Unions and their members have shared in the progress of the company through a relationship of mutual respect, for the most part amiable. However, there have been work stoppages, including the idling of several thousand production workers in main plants of the St. Paul area for two months in 1967 during the first strike in their history.

The relationship of fairness and respect with one union official was notably long-lasting. Production employee Joseph E. Karth in 1948 was elected president of CIO Local 75, which later became the OCAW (Oil, Chemical and Atomic Workers) local representing some St. Paul workers.

Karth had been with 3M since 1941, except for a military leave of absence during World War II. After his 1948-58 union duties he received another leave of

"An American working in Thailand must make rapid adjustment," says Fred Harris, former financial staff member who became managing director, 3M Thailand, where he's learning a new language. One of his daughters was born in Bangkok.*

Research scientists, sales personnel and computer programmers
sit side by side in 3M symphony. To the right, at make-up
mirrors are Elaine Merrill, Traffic Control Materials,
John Gagnon of Central Research and others from four 3M musical groups
preparing for an annual, free-to-the-public Christmas concert.

absence for public service when he was elected to the U.S. Congress from Minnesota's Fourth District. In 18 years as a Congressman, he found himself representing many more 3Mers than in his early contract negotiations. And he still found himself occasionally in discussions with 3M officials in Washington to testify on trade or tax legislation.

All long-service employees share in the honors and recognition extended during annual service-award programs, where long-term employees and their husbands or wives gather with management to observe landmarks in their careers.

Typically, employees are challenged as well as cheered at these events.

"Let's review your qualifications," said Robert N. Wolfe, group vice president and 3M director, to Service Award participants in Bristol, Pennsylvania, where he had served as plant manager earlier in his career.

"You are at the peak of your powers as a contributing member of society. You've never been smarter. You've never had more experience than you have right now. You have witnessed social change never before seen in history and you were a part of that.

"As graduate students in the school of hard knocks, you

have power—and responsibility—on and off the job. Your youthful colleagues—even your youthful critics—take their cues from you. Their attitudes toward themselves, their jobs and their roles in life are profoundly influenced by the attitudes that you project."

The spirit of "The Mining" which is reflected in the Service Award ceremonies extends into retirement.

"I know it's trite to talk about the 3M 'family'," commented one retiree, "but even after four years I feel as though I'm part of the company, and I keep in close touch." Many retirees maintain an active relationship with 3M long after their pension programs are arranged and long after they receive their gold wallet cards which identify them as Goodwill Ambassadors, with the privilege of participating in 3M activities and sharing recreational facilities.

Several times retired 3Mers have been granted increases in pension to help them combat inflation and many of them have expressed special appreciation for the continuing relationship with their company.

"Thanks to all the 3Mers of today who continue to make these things possible," they said in sum. E. Donald Patterson, Brooklyn Center, Minnesota, wrote, "The appreciation is two-fold. The extra money is always welcome, but equally important is being remembered and still considered part of the 3M family."

"3M . . . still hasn't forgotten us old-timers who can remember the days when we knew almost every employee by first name," said Kyran Dougherty, Fort Lauderdale, Florida.

Many old timers recall with nostalgia the days of company-wide warmth and intimacy, which still remains evident especially within the smaller operating units. The related traditions remain steadfast since first set forth by McKnight decades ago. A former 3Mer referred to these traditions as "unwritten policies which add much to the flavor and fervor of the company."

The willingness to tolerate mistakes, for example, is not set forth in the management guide or the office operating manual, but it's ingrained in the fiber of a company which recognizes that people will stumble on occasion, but only if they're in motion.

Senior pilot plant technician David Alm handles materials in a glass reactor distillation system, allowing storage, use and disposal of chemicals without human contact.

Mother's helper: engineering specialist Dick deNeui tests an applicator which automatically applies 3M tape to baby diapers for safe, simpler infant care.

One 3M executive expressed it this way: "It's my conviction that we learn more from our mistakes than we do from our successes," he said. "However, we should not take mistakes lightly and we should be creative in making mistakes. We've learned nothing if we make the same mistake twice."

On the same theme, Jack Whitcomb, retired director, recalls his experience as a young manager in the abrasives division. "I pulled a real boner," he said, "and I figured I'd better get to March's office [Cecil C. March, then group vice president] and take my lumps.

"When I told him that I had made a mistake, he just looked at me for a minute and then he said, 'Just a minute . . . I approved your project and if there was a mistake, *we* made it together.' "

While 3M makes and markets some 600 varieties of tape, its antipathy for "red tape" has not changed over the years. Bigness, of course, brings some dictums and decrees, some do's and don'ts, but resistance to formalized rules and regulations continues strong.

Like most companies, 3M has organization charts, but the blocks stay on the charts, and don't become roadblocks in getting the job done. The same can be said for position descriptions. "We want them to outline the job, not confine it," explained a former personnel vice president.

Speaking to 3M marketing associates in 1976, Lew Lehr stated it this way: "Certainly we need job descriptions, but when you attempt to put a fence around the pasture and call it 'marketing,' for example, or 'research,' all you do is turn the people in the pasture into sheep—or you attract only sheep. That's not what we want. We want innovativeness and creativity, aimed at serving people's needs."

At 3M innovativeness and creativity result in opportunity, as noted by Ray Herzog at an annual meeting of stockholders. "In one recent five-year period," he said, "new general managers were named in two-thirds of our three dozen operating units. And these promotions were the result of growth not turnover." Herzog also noted that during the same period 22 of 27 marketing directors were newly appointed, as were 20 of 24 manufacturing directors, and 21 of 28 technical directors.

Relaxing with his family is Jon D. Hovde, injured veteran of Vietnam who works in the Hardware-Paint Trades division.

Reducing it all
to one word: opportunity

"The success of these hundred or so people," he concluded "is only part of the story, because every time one of them is promoted, dozens of other jobs open up, making promotions possible for other people.

"If I could reduce all of this to one word, it would have to be opportunity."

Whether written or unwritten, many policies for individual development are rooted deeply in 3M's heritage. Promotion comes from within and there is no favoritism for relatives in hiring or promotions. The latter policy was initiated by McKnight because, as the story goes, he lost a promotion early in his career to the office manager's son. For many decades, McKnight and succeeding members of executive management have firmly supported these policies, convinced that employees on the firing line should be encouraged and recognized.

Encouragement, of course, can be subtle and informal like a warm, first-name telephone response from an executive who more often than not takes his own phone calls. Or a thank you note from a supervisor for a job well done. Or a promotion picture in the employee publications.

One security guard might also agree that encouragement is a pat on the back from the board chairman. A newly hired plant guard refused to admit McKnight to a tape factory because he didn't have his employee pass.

Another employee who was with McKnight was incredulous. "Don't you know that's Mr. McKnight," he whispered.

"I'm sorry," the guard responded, "but he still has to have a pass."

McKnight left without comment, but returned later with his pass and warmly complimented the guard for doing his job.

Linda Rowley and Margaret Lang agree that encouragement—and recognition—can extend beyond daily, on-the-job good fellowship and informality. A staffing department interviewer, Rowley saw the company's tuition refund program as an opportunity to make her own luck. She has spent more than three years in night classes at the University of Minnesota and at Lakewood Community College, working toward a degree in Business Administration with an accounting major.

"My bosses have encouraged me to keep up my night school efforts," she acknowledged, "and my last boss was grooming me to take over his job. Without the tuition refund program, it would not have been possible."

Rowley received her promotion when Howard Huerth, her supervisor, retired.

After several years as a production worker at the New Ulm, Minnesota Electro Products plant, Margaret Lang decided to improve her education and her career opportunities. She enrolled in night classes at Mankato State University, some 28 miles from New Ulm, and for the next five years logged thousands of miles and burned considerable "midnight oil" while working toward her degree.

Lang's own perseverance along with, as she explained, "a lot of support from friends and 3M's tuition refund," have resulted in her promotion to a salaried position in quality control at the same New Ulm plant.

3M's tuition refund program is but one of the formal programs through which the company encourages development on the job. They range from craft apprenticeships to specialized training in manufacturing, technical service, sales, engineering and data processing, to mention a few. Specialists in education and training provide staff support and expertise to all areas of 3M and offer courses during working hours for personal development and supervisory-management instruction.

Personal development has a high priority at 3M where talent, creativity and managerial abilities are necessary ingredients to fuel the company's growth, and where managers and supervisors understand that one of their duties is to prepare their people for greater responsibilities. Supervisors complete periodic "appraisals" and "estimates of potential" evaluating each individual's performance and progress, and readiness for new challenges.

Supporting such development programs is a human resource system which keeps track of 3M people who because of their performance, abilities and perhaps special skills are available for promotion wherever the company may need their strengths.

"We do a great deal of our own training and personnel

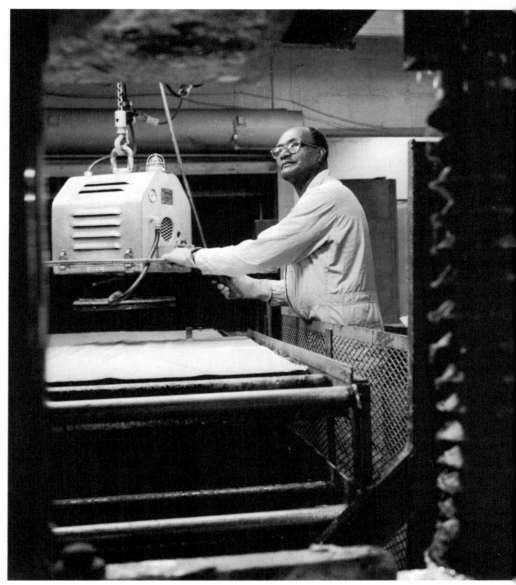

Laminator press operator George Johnson, a 3M Factory Training Center graduate, works with reinforced plastics.

development," Lew Lehr explained to a college audience, "but the enthusiasm, dedication and self-learning the individual does is the key to his or her ultimate success."

Linda Rowley, Margaret Lang and hundreds of other 3M employees would concur.

There are other keys to success at 3M, depending upon each individual's personal career objective. Jack Warosh, for example, was a Packaging Systems salesman out of Denver, Colorado, when he was offered an opportunity as sales manager in another part of the country. His roots ran deep in Denver, however, and he elected to turn down the promotion.

He continued to serve his territory well from his Colorado base, accepting an additional assignment as field sales trainer where his experience and expertise are shared with young salesmen. Rather than moving to sales

management, he climbed another side of 3M's dual ladder to the position of account executive, joining an elite group of close to 100 U.S. sales representatives to be so recognized.

"The challenge—and the reward," said Jack, "have been fitted to my qualifications. I appreciate that."

Dr. John Wetz, a technical specialist, is a statistical consultant in Information Systems & Data Processing. He unscrambles problems dealing with the full variety of corporate units: manufacturing, legal, sales, marketing. Unencumbered by administrative chores, he devotes full time to being a statistical "answer man," with "no chance of ever becoming bored, because the problems are so varied and so immense."

A 13-year 3Mer, Wetz also has a master's degree in Chemical Engineering. While serving as chairman of the education committee of the local chapter of the American

Research specialist William C. Flanagan, executive scientist Dr. James R. Johnson and corporate scientist Dr. George V. D. Tiers oblige a visiting artist, in foreground, by showing how toner powder can be used to finish off a print.

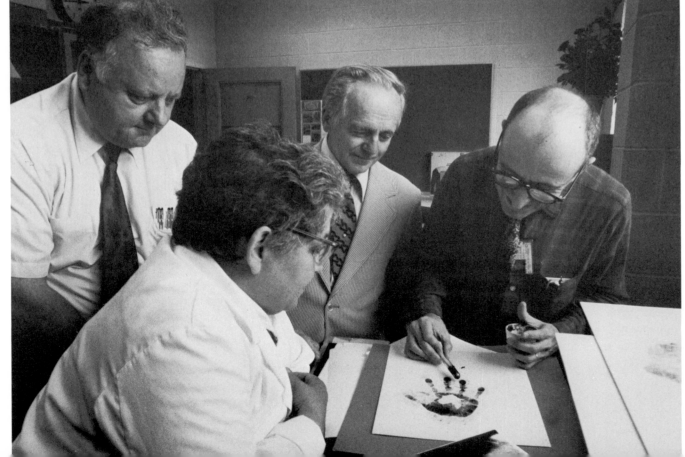

Society for Quality Control, he helped institute a new program of study to train quality technicians at St. Paul's Technical Vocational Institute.

Encouraging employees to find their own career paths, to do their own thing and their own thinking, is also one of the keys to 3M's success. Ray Herzog explains it this way:

"We try to spread the decision making so that people can control their own destinies. And we don't allow talent to dry up through fear of occasional failure. This is the way I've enjoyed 3M. I think it's the way all our old-timers enjoyed 3M and I think it's the way our newcomers are going to enjoy 3M."

Herzog's words explain in part why 3M processes thousands upon thousands of job applications, in good times or bad, from young and old, men and women, experienced and inexperienced. And they explain also why 3M was singled out by *Money* magazine as one of "Ten Terrific Companies to Work For," based on the magazine's survey in 1976 of 32 recruiting firms. Other companies on the list included IBM, Eastman Kodak, Du Pont, Procter & Gamble, GE, Xerox.

Money reported that the results showed "a definite leaning toward companies with room for many kinds of people, in itself a mark of a good place to work."

It concluded by noting that the recruiters' comments led consistently to certain other conclusions . . . "Excellence in their products, research, marketing, management and people . . . and sensitivity to human problems."

Company success, of course, stems from products and services that help solve human problems. That's 3M's number one social contribution. In the process, though, combined talents and resources of the corporation permit 3M to reach out and help society in additional ways that most individuals could not afford.

One 3M Foundation commitment is for $1.5 million, pledged toward a new Center for the Science Museum of Minnesota. A half-million-dollar pledge to a new Mayo Medical School was fulfilled by 3M over a five-year period. Educational grants account for almost half of 3M's philanthropy in a typical year, and include grants to private college funds in 30 states.

Fund drives for numerous community agencies are supported by 3M and its people—with time and talent, as

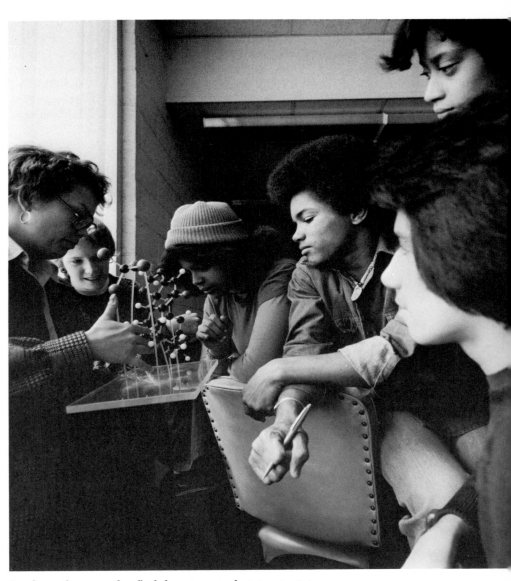

Students from a school's laboratory technician training program examine a model of an organic compound with Cheryl Jones of the Industrial Mineral Products division. Jones teaches some of the classes.

well as money—in more than 75 locations around the United States.

This social sensitivity is also evidenced in a variety of employee-help programs, to deal with problems ranging from emotional stress to chemical dependency to the trials of relocation. For example, 3M's rehabilitation program for alcoholics, which predates many state programs, has been adopted by other companies with which 3M has shared its experiences.

With job opportunities in 50 states, 46 countries and six continents, some employees on occasion think of 3M as "Minnesota Mining and Moving Company." But most people's problems in long-distance relocations pale in contrast to the odyssey of the Henry Mai family. In the final days of the Vietnam war, Mai was one of 30 Saigon 3Mers who had plane tickets for his entire family. But there was no plane.

Resourceful and persistent, Mai and his family took to an open boat and following one harrowing experience after another, finally succeeded in reaching Japan. There he was reunited with 3M and the company was able to expedite a transfer, first to Guam, then to California and finally to St. Paul.

"They arrived in St. Paul with nothing but the clothes on their backs," said Arnie Dickson, office manager, International Operations. "Two of the women from the office and I took the family shopping for clothes, then lodged them temporarily in a local motel before getting them into a home."

The five children and Mrs. Mai were tutored in English through the 3M Language Society and the three older children entered the University of Minnesota. Mai himself was promoted to an Electrical Products marketing position.

Other 3Mers sometimes need help of other kinds. Programs to rehabilitate disabled employees and efforts to hire the handicapped both have as their aim the full use of human resources.

"The company's continued growth demands that we seek out and hire all the talents available to us, as needed," says Carlos W. Luis, a one-time factory employee serving as vice president for public affairs and personnel relations in 3M's anniversary year.

"We simply cannot afford," he says, "to do without those individuals who have so much to contribute to our company and to the larger society of which we are a part."

This active philosophy applies to affirmative action in equal employment opportunity for anyone who seeks to join the company.

"I didn't think 3M would hire a grandmother," said Hazel Dahme, grandmother of eight and foster parent to 65 children over an 18-year period. She was no stranger to work when she applied for a job with 3M in Aberdeen, South Dakota. An average of 42 diapers a day is a reality any parent can appreciate.

"Now, with all the foster children gone, I'm grateful for the stimulation of my job as a finisher operator, and for all my new friends. I hope I'm not a bad influence on the younger people I work with," she joked, "for they have a good effect on me."

Hazel Dahme's observation is stated many different ways by new employees—and even some old-timers—who discover or rediscover that the ability, skill or talent they need to solve a problem or to exploit an opportunity is as close as a phone call in the interoffice directory. "What I like about 3M," said a three-year marketing employee, "is all the people available to help. What I like even more is the cheerful and pleasant way help is offered."

William L. McKnight, the $11.55 per week assistant bookkeeper who advanced to become 3M board chairman, may have said it best when reviewing his 65-year relationship with the company:

"It is proper to emphasize how much we depend on each other. Our challenge, while stressing this important lesson of humanity, lies in maintaining, at the same time, a proper respect for the individual. We lose something valuable if we uproot all notion of personal self-reliance and the dignity of work . . .

"To continue our progress and service to America and the world, we need a healthy appreciation of those who exercise the free man's option for excellence, permitting the creation of something for all of us, enriching lives with new ideas and products.

"The best and hardest work is done in the spirit of adventure and challenge." □

Recharging for the next shift: Battery room electrician John Reiners and materials-handling truck serviceman Charles Cermak.

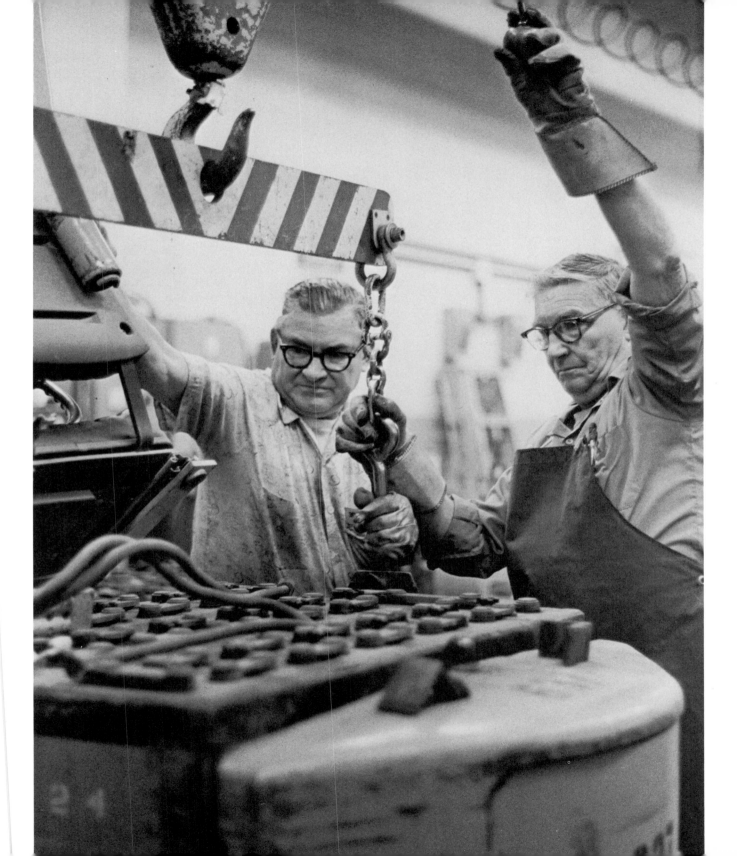

Acknowledgements

In recording these few chapters of the continuing 3M story, we relied heavily on the insights and experiences of the following 3M retirees. We gratefully acknowledge their help.

William H. Abbott
Robert L. Ackerberg
Robert W. Adam
Alvin W. Boese
John A. Borden
John A. Brown
Calvin H. Corwin
Bert S. Cross
Donald J. Douglas
Richard G. Drew
Joseph C. Duke
Roy J. Gavin
Marion Gould
Irwin R. Hansen
Melvin C. Hegdal
George Heideman
Harry Heltzer
Truman J. Henley
Robert V. Holton
Mildred Jacobsen
Clifford L. Jewett
Herbert D. Johnson
Edward J. Kane

Roy W. Keeley
James Keith
Harold Kinney
D. W. Maher
William L. McKnight
Robert W. Mueller
George Netherly
Maynard H. Patterson
Cyril P. Pesek
A. E. Raymond
Alan H. Redpath
Clarence B. Sampair
Richard L. Sheppard
George W. Swenson
Arthur K. Telfer
Hubert J. Tierney
Robert H. Tucker
William A. Vievering
Walter E. Vroman
Charles W. Walton
Robert L. Westbee
Louis F. Weyand
John F. Whitcomb

Special credit also belongs to a number of employees throughout the company for their help with the research, writing, review, editing, photography and manuscript work that went into this anniversary volume. "Our Story" has been published largely as a result of their efforts and performance, often beyond the press of regular duties.

We wish to acknowledge the help we had from Robert N. Taylor, who designed this book, and from Warren Feist and Charles Mangel, whose counsel and editorial assistance were enlisted. Certainly an earlier volume, "The Brand of the Tartan" by Virginia Huck, served as an essential resource.

John J. Verstraete
Vice President, Public Relations
3M Company